Y0-BDI-924

חובות הלבבות
שער יחוד המעשה, הכניעה, והתשובה

Duties of the Heart
The Gates of Dedication of Purpose, Humility and Repentance

Translated and Annotated by
Avraham Yaakov Finkel

YESHIVATH BETH MOSHE
SCRANTON, PA.

Yeshivath Beth Moshe
930 Hickory Street, Scranton, PA 18505
(717) 346-1747

First Edition

ISBN 0-892692-00-7

CONTENTS

הקדמה
מהראש ישיבה
מורינו הרב יעקב שניידמאן שליט״א

בהגיע ימי התשובה ראוי תחילה להתבונן על עניני יחוד המעשה והכניעה שהם עיקר ההכנות לתשובה ע״כ צירפנו כאחד אלו השלשה שערים מספר חובות הלבבות.

והנה מסורת בני ישיבה להתחיל לימוד ספר חובת הלבבות משער יחוד המעשה. ונראה לתת שלשה טעמים לזה. אחד, בשער הזה מבאר המחבר בדיוק גדול כחות הנפש בבני אדם. וכל הלומד ומעמיק בדבריו נדמה לו כאילו מדבר אליו בדוקא, והוא מבאר מלחמת הנפש שכולנו לוחמים ומדריכנו איך לנצח. ונמצא דהוא הקדמה לכל דרכי האדם, אם לעשות או לא לעשות וגם איך יעשה ומה יהיה מחשבתו בשעת עשייתו. מובן מאליו גודל נחיצות לימוד השער הזה.

שנית, מבואר בש״ס בכמה מקומות שחז״ל עשו תקנות וסייגים, וכולם לחזק קיום המצות ואיסורי התורה. ולפעמים אדם משתומם על התקנה ושואל בלבו וכי יש לחוש חששה רחוקה כזה עד שהוצרכו לעשות תקנה. וחס ושלום נוכל לבא להרהר אחר דברי חז״ל. לימוד השער הזה הוא תיקון גדול להרהורים כאלה. דהרי המחבר מציע לפנינו בדרך ויכוח בין היצר והאדם כל ההסתות ומ־חשבות הנולדות בדעת האדם להפריע אותו מעבודתו. ובאמת מה שעשה המחבר הוא פלא גדול שאסף בשער קטן כזה כמעט כל מה שיכול לעלות על הדעת להפריע האדם מעבודת בוראו. ומי יחשוב כזה שידע איך לקלע אל המטרה. וע״כ אדם הלומד שער זה יודה לעצמו שרק אדם גדול אשר יש בו רוח הקדש יכול לחבר שער כזה

ונפש האדם היתה פתוחה אצלו כספר פתוח שראה הכל בדיוק. ואם להמחבר היה כך, קל וחומר לחז״ל שהיו כמה דורות לפניו, והמחבר הרי יסד דבריו על דבריהם, ודאי ידעו והבינו נפש האדם כאספקל-ריא המאירה. ועל פי הך ידיעה וברוח קדשם תקנו תקנות להרחיק אדם מן העבירה ולחזק אותו בקיום המצות.

שלישית, דבר גדול חידש לנו המחבר, במה שסידר השער כויכוח בין האדם עצמו עם היצר כאילו היצר הוא חוץ לאדם ובא להסיתו, ומזה יש ללמוד עיקר גדול. דהרי כשאנו לוחמים נגד היצר רוב פעמים אין אנו חושבים בעצמנו שהיצר נכנס בנפשנו להסות. ובדעתנו כל הצדדים הם צדדי נפשותינו, דיש לנו רצון כזה ויש לנו רצון כנגד. והמדע המדרני מיוסד על זה שהאדם ימלא רצון נפשו ישתכח הדבר. ומסידור המחבר נלמד יסוד הראשון במלחמת היצר שהוא לידע דהאלקים ברא את האדם ישר, והיצר מכנס בו חשבונות רבות.

ובאמת יסוד זה מבואר בהרמב״ם בפרק ב׳ מהלכות גירושין הלכה כ׳ וז״ל, מי שהדין נותן שכופין אותו לגרש וכו׳ בית דין של ישראל וכו׳ מכין אותו עד שיאמר רוצה אני וכו׳ ולמה לא בטל גט זה שהרי הוא אונס וכו׳ שאין אומרים אונס אלא למי שנלחץ ונדחק לעשות דבר שאינו מחויב מן התורה וכו׳ אבל מי שתקפו יצרו הרע לבטל מצוה או לעשות עבירה והוכה עד שעשה דבר שחייב לעשותו וכו׳ אין זה אנוס ממנו אלא הוא אנס עצמו בדעתו הרע וכו׳ וכיון שהוכה עד שתשש יצרו ואמר רוצה אני כבר גרש לרצונו וכו׳. ע״כ. וגילה לנו הרמב״ם דמה שהאדם מתעקש שלא לעשות הוא כח היצר שנכנס בו. ונקח משל מתינוק שרוצה דבר שאינו טוב לו. והוא שואג וכועס וכמעט יוצא מדעתו בשביל שרוצה אותו דבר עד שאביו מכה אותו. ועל ידי זה מתיש יצרו ושוב יכולים לדבר אליו. וברור לנו שהתינוק לאותו שעה יוצא מדעתו ואין זה עצמיותו. ואנו כמו כן בשעת חימום החטא יוצאין מדעתינו עד שלפעמים רק על ידי הכאה יותש יצרנו. הרי מבואר עיקר גדול במהלך התורה איך ינהג האדם במלחמתו נגד היצר, והוא להכיר דאין היצר עצמיותו ואדרבה הוא מסיתנו לעבור על רצוננו לעבוד לבוראנו. הי״ת יסיר ממנו הסתות היצר ויראנו הדרך לעבודתו.

TRANSLATION OF RABBI YAAKOV SCHNAIDMAN'S PROLOGUE

As we approach the Days of Repentance it is fitting to study the ideals of dedication of purpose and humility because they are necessary for repentance. We therefore combined these three gates in this volume.

There is also a tradition to begin studying *Duties of the Heart* with the "Gate of Dedication of Purpose." We can offer three reasons for this.

The First: The author analyses in depth the psyche of people. Anyone studying this work realizes that his own self is being addressed. The inner conflict of man is detailed and a plan for success is offered. This is a prerequisite for all our actions. We are taught how to act when commanded and to desist from the temptation of the *yetzer hara*. We are also taught how to control our thoughts when involved in the Service of God.

The Second: We find in the Talmud that our Sages enacted numerous decrees and protective legislation to safeguard the Torah. At times, one wonders if the concerns that our Sages had were probable enough to require the enactment of such legislation. Studying the gate of "Dedication of Purpose", we see that the forces of man's intellect were revealed to the author like an open book. This section which addresses all the possible wiles the evil inclination uses to deter us from serving our Creator, makes us realize that this could only have been written with Divine Inspiration. Our Sages, from whom the author based his words, surely had even a clearer picture of man's intellect. It is with this knowledge and Divine Inspiration that they enacted legislation to distance us from sin and strengthen us to fulfill the mitzvos.

The Third: The author arranged this section as a dialogue between man and his evil inclination, portraying the evil inclination as separate and apart from man himself. From this we see that many of our thoughts and impulses are not an integral part of ourselves, rather they come from the evil inclination. This is in contrast to modern thought that everyone must fulfill his desires. We must realize that man's intellect is pure but the evil inclination feeds him foreign ideas.

We see a directive to understand that the evil inclination is not an integral part of ourselves.This idea is stated clearly in the Rambam. Although one cannot divorce his wife under duress, when a Jewish court forces a man to divorce his wife, the divorce is valid. Rambam explains that a Jew inherently wants to do the proper thing, he is only refusing because he being compelled by the evil inclination. The pressure brought on him by the court is only to free him from the pressure of the evil inclination; he then acts of his own will which is to do the right thing.

Analogous to this is a child who wants something that is harmful to his health. He screams, nearly going out of his mind with rage, until he is punished by his parent and comes back to his senses. So too, at times, the evil inclination confronts us and we literally lose our minds and need the punishment of the court to bring us to our senses.

May God remove the temptations of the evil inclination from us and show us the proper path to serve Him.

DUTIES OF THE HEART

GATE FIVE

The Gate of Dedicating Our Actions to God

Why All Our Actions Should Be Dedicated to God's Name, and Why We Should Avoid Hypocrisy

INTRODUCTION

Having explained in the previous Gate the concept of trusting God, we thought it advisable to follow with a discussion of the duty to dedicate all our acts only to God. This path of action will bring you to purge your thoughts and purify your heart so that you won't act out of confusion, and you will rid yourself of the urge to curry favor with others which leads to hypocrisy and flattery. Elihu, [the companion of Iyov], put it this way, *I would not show regard for any man, or temper my speech for anyone's sake. For I do not know how to temper my speech (Iyov 32:21,22)*.

We will discuss six points concerning dedicating our actions to God:

One: What is meant by "Dedicating ones actions to God".

Two: How to dedicate one's actions to God.

Three: Which acts must be dedicated to God.

Four: Things that deter you from dedicating your actions to G-d.

Five: How to stave off the blandishments of the *yetzer hara*.

Six: The obligation to guard and control your thoughts.

CHAPTER ONE

What Is Meant By "Dedicating One's Actions to God"

Dedicating one's actions to God means that whenever one serves God—either publicly or privately—his intentions are for the sake of His Name alone, and not to impress others.

CHAPTER TWO

How To Dedicate One's Actions to God

There are ten steps one must take to dedicate his actions to God. When these ten steps are anchored in his heart, and become the cornerstone of his service to God and the root of his actions, he will be able to dedicate his actions to God. This means he will turn to no one but Him, expect no one but Him to fulfill his wishes, and he will want only to please God.

The ten steps are: (1) to accept wholeheartedly the Oneness of God; (2) to be aware of the kindness God constantly bestows on him; (3) to accept upon himself the service of God; (4) to recognize the need to trust God alone rather than anyone else; (5) to believe that no one can help or harm him without the Creator's approval; (6) to be indifferent to praise and insult; (7) to refrain from trying to ingratiate himself with people; (8) to divert his attention from worldly matters when he is occupied with concerns of the World to Come; (9) to be in awe of God and feel ashamed before Him; (10) to be guided by his intellect and accept its advice when the *yetzer hara* is trying to sway him.

CHAPTER THREE

Which Acts Must Be Dedicated to God

Duties of the limbs—tangible mitzvos such as wearing tefillin, eating matzah and taking the lulav in hand—which we do in order to fulfill God's will, become perfected by being dedicated to the service of God. It is possible to do these mitzvos for a purpose other than for the sake of God. For example, a person might do them to impress other people [with his piety], hoping to gain their respect and praise.

However, *duties of the heart*, [such as, believing in Hashem, loving Him, fearing Him, trusting Him and loving your neighbor] can not be done insincerely to gain respect or praise, because no one, [other than God], knows what is in one's heart when he does them. You do these mitzvos only for the sake of the Creator, the One Who scrutinizes the innermost recesses of your soul. As it says, *I, Hashem, plumb the feelings and search the innermost thoughts (Yirmeyah 17:10)*, and, *The hidden things belong to Hashem, our God (Devarim 29:28).*

CHAPTER FOUR

Things That Deter You From Dedicating Your Actions to God

There are three things that keep a person from dedicating his actions to God:

One: Failure to grasp the [exalted majesty] of God and His abundant goodness.

Two: Failure to understand His mitzvos and His Torah.

Three: The enticements of the *yetzer hara*—evil inclination—which make the empty pleasures of this world seem alluring and thereby discourage one from taking the road that leads to the World to Come.

Ignorance of God's exaltedness detracts one from dedicated service because a person cannot serve his Master wholeheartedly if he is not completely conscious of Him. One serves someone only if he expects reward or punishment. If one serves God without recognizing His greatness, he is not motivated by his sincerity in his service to the Creator but rather by the impression he makes on people. He is afraid of people or he hopes to benefit from them, [thus he tries to impress them with feigned piety]. He is serving man rather than man's Creator.

This same lack of comprehending God is also the root cause for idolatry. But in fact the conduct of an idol worshipper is less reprehensible than that of the hypocrite, [who pretends to serve God but is actually serving people], for four reasons:

One: The idol worshippers of old, lived in a time when there were no prophets to warn them through signs and wonders that their beliefs were false. [They therefore had no way of knowing that they were on the wrong path.] By contrast, a person who observes the Torah for the wrong motive is accountable because he has already accepted [from the Torah] the mitzvos and the service of God, and has been cautioned not to serve anyone else.

Two: An idolater, worships things [like statues, trees, the sun and planets] that do not rebel against God, whereas a person who observe's God's Torah to impress people, worships these people, some of whom are not observant and are actually rebelling against God.

Three: An idol worshipper serves only one idol, whereas the hypocrite serves an endless number of people [in his hunger for their approval and admiration].

Four: An idolater's pagan way of worship is obvious, so people can be alerted to stay away from his public denial of God. On the other hand, the hypocrite's denial of God is not apparent, therefore people trust and learn from him. He can do much more harm than an idol worshipper. In fact, hypocrisy is the world's worst disease; in our language we call such an individual a *hypocrite*, a *braggart*, and a *seducer*.

[Failure to understand the commandments of the Torah detracts one from dedicating his actions to God,] because one who does not understand his directives, cannot be doing them with complete dedication. He will not perform any act because of God's commandment but rather for some other reason. This is so, even if he is conscious of God and His greatness. Our Sages put it this way, *A boor cannot be fearful of sin; an unlearned person cannot be scrupulously pious (Avos 2:5).*

The seductive ideas of the *yetzer hara* fall into two categories:

One: The *yetzer hara* raises doubt in a person's mind about fundamental beliefs [like prophecy, reward and punishment,] and undermines his faith so that he won't do even one mitzvah with the intent of serving God.

Two: The *yetzer hara* offers arguments to "prove" that you are not required to serve God enthusiastically and zealously, that you don't need to exert yourself in His service, and that you should devote your energies toward the welfare of this world and its inhabitants.

CHAPTER FIVE

How to Stave Off the Blandishments of the *Yetzer Hara*

It is worthwhile to offer a few examples of the tactics the *yetzer hara* uses [to seduce you], so that you may guard against them and be able to serve God wholeheartedly. As the wise King Solomon said, *The wise man, hearing them, will gain more wisdom; the discerning man will acquire strategies (Mishlei 1:5).*

My friend, be aware that the greatest enemy you have in the world is your *yetzer hara*. It is an integral part of you, inextricably fused with your spiritual essence. The *yetzer hara* joins you in governing your physical and spiritual senses and rules over the secrets of your soul and the darkest recesses of your heart. It has a recommendation to you on every public or private move you make and waits for the chance to entice you every step you take. You may be unaware of it [and unsuspecting of its tricks], but it is aware of you [and plans to entrap you]. You ignore it, but it never ignores you. The *yetzer hara* pretends to be your friend, adorns itself with a robe of love, and passes itself off as your trusted companion, counselor, and closest friend. It will signal and wave to you, and act as if it is rushing to fulfill your wishes, while in reality, it is shooting poisoned arrows to destroy you. As it says, *Like a madman scattering firebrands, arrows and lethal objects, is one who cheats his fellow and then says, 'I was only joking' (Mishlei 26:18,19).*

The most powerful weapon in the *yetzer hara's* arsenal, is its attempt to sow doubt in your mind about your beliefs. It tries to create uncertainty about things that are clear to you; to confuse your mind with false ideas and misleading arguments in order to steer you away from doing good and make you doubt your faith.

If you are wary and prepared to fight with your mind's weapons, you will be safe, with God's help. But if you allow it to run your life and follow its lead, it will not let go until it has destroyed you in both worlds and expelled you from both dwelling places. As it says about one example [of the *yetzer hara's* schemes] and about one of its warriors, *For many are those she has struck dead, and numerous are her victims. Her house is a highway to the nether world, leading down to death's inner chambers (Mishlei 7:26,27).*

Don't be sidetracked from your battle with the *yetzer hara*; don't fight anyone or anything other than the *yetzer hara*. Don't let a struggle against a distant enemy take your attention away from your struggle against the one that never leaves you. Don't let attacks by someone who can accost you only with the Creator's permission keep you from repelling attacks by the *yetzer hara* who does not need permission to accost you.

There once was a righteous man who met a group of soldiers returning triumphantly from the battlefield, carrying a rich haul of captured booty. He said to them, "You have come back from winning a minor battle; but the big battle is still ahead of you!"

"What big battle are you talking about?" the soldiers asked.

"The battle against the *yetzer hara* and his legions," the righteous man replied.

An enemy you defeated once or twice leaves you alone and does not dream of attacking you again. Because he realizes that you are stronger than he is, he gives up the idea of defeating you. The *yetzer hara*, however, does not care whether it was defeated once or a hundred times, or even if it defeated you, or you defeated it. For it knows that if it defeats you, it will destroy you [spiritually], and if you defeat it once, it will lie in wait for you the rest of your life. As our Sages said, *Do not believe in yourself until the day you die (Avos 2:4)*. Even the smallest victory is important to the *yetzer hara*, for he knows that the small victory is a rung on the ladder toward greater victories. Therefore it is important to watch out from it and not to give in to any of its wishes.

Think of your smallest victory over the *yetzer hara* as a major achievement, for this small victory is a stepping stone toward greater triumphs.

The *yetzer hara* is quick to trap you, but if you stand up to it, it will be quick to do your bidding and powerless to resist you. As it says, *"Its desire is toward you, but you can be its master" (Bereishis 4:7).*

Don't be intimidated by the *yetzer hara*, no matter how many troops it has; don't be afraid, no matter how many allies it can muster. Its main goal is to prove that falsehood is truth; its major objective is to demonstrate that deception is honesty. It is easy to shatter the *yetzer hara*, if you recognize this weakness. As the wise King Solomon phrased it, *There was a little city, with few inhabitants in it; and to it came a great king, who surrounded it and built mighty siege works against it. Present in the city was a poor wise man who saved the city with his wisdom. Yet no one remembered that poor man (Koheles 9:14).*

Man is compared to *a little city*, because man is a miniature universe. His limbs and character traits are referred to as *few inhabitants*, because they are few in comparison to man's insatiable appetites, his constant cravings and his inability to satisfy them. The *yetzer hara* is portrayed as *a great king*, because of its armies, attendants and staff. It is said to *surround the city*, because the *yetzer hara* affects all facets of your public and private life. It is described as having *built mighty siege works against it*, because the *yetzer hara* tries to destroy man through evil thoughts, fantasies, and shameful deeds, as we will explain further on in this gate, with God's help. The phrase, *Present in the city was a wise man* refers to the human intellect, which is characterized as *poor* because it has only very few helpers and supporters. This explains why it says, *no one remembered that poor man* and in the next verse, *the poor man's wisdom is despised.*

[This parable, of the battle that rages between the intellect and the *yetzer hara*], teaches us, that despite the intellect's weakness, if it makes a stand, the *yetzer hara* surrenders, and he can ward off the harm the *yetzer hara* is trying to inflict. A little truth drives away a lot of falsehood, just as a little bit of light drives away a lot of darkness.

This parable should encourage you to subdue your cravings and resist the blandishments of the *yetzer hara* with vigor and diligence. For the *yetzer hara* is powerless and rapidly fades away when faced by reason. As it says, *Evildoers will grovel before good people (Mishlei 14:19).*

Doubt About the Immortality of the Soul

The *yetzer hara* begins its nefarious pursuit by encouraging you to believe that the soul cannot survive without the body, and therefore perishes when the body dies. It offers baseless and spurious arguments, as become obvious when you analyze them. Its aim is to encourage you to indulge in fleeting thrills and worldly delights. It tries to convince you to join the chorus of the pleasure-seekers who say, "*Eat and drink, for tomorrow we die!*" *(Yeshayah 22:13)*. But if you compare the *yetzer hara*'s arguments to the words of the prophets, or the writings of the early thinkers you will stand aloof from the *yetzer hara*.

Doubt About the Creator

When the *yetzer hara* cannot make you doubt the immortality of the soul, it will try to make you question the existence of God. It will say that the world did not have a beginning and was never created, that it never was different nor will be different from what it is now. It will say that there is neither a Creator, nor was anything ever created; no one is obligated to worship anything, because everything is equally primordial and timeless. If the *yetzer hara* comes to you with these heresies, your common sense and Scriptural verse will make you see their fallacies, as we discussed in the chapter on God's unity in the first gate of this book wherein we proved that the world has a Creator who created it out of nothing.

Doubt About God's Unity

When the *yetzer hara* cannot make you doubt [the existence of God], it will try to make you stumble with the idea that God has associates. It will advocate the belief of dualism, or the notion that nature is divine, or the theories of the half-witted astrologers and the like. But when you understand what we explained above in the Gate of God's Oneness—that God is One and timeless—these fallacies will fall by the wayside.

Doubt About the Need to Serve God

When the *yetzer hara* despairs of making you believe these falsehoods, it tries to convince you not to serve the Creator. It tells you it makes sense to serve someone only if your service is needed. Since the Creator does not need the service of the people He created, there is no need to serve Him. These doubts will vanish into thin air when you reflect upon God's kindness to you and your obligation to serve Him, as we discussed in the Gate of Reflection and the Gate of Service to God.

Doubts About the Torah

When the *yetzer hara* cannot persuade you to stop serving God, it tries to raise uncertainty in your mind about prophecy, the prophets, the truth of the Torah, and whether we must believe it [and fulfill its commandments]. Let reason be your guide and fight the *yetzer hara* with the arguments outlined in the Gate of Service to God and those doubts will disappear. You will recognize that prophecy is genuine, that the prophets spoke in the name of God, that God sent Moshe to give us the Torah, and that, consequently, we are required to observe the Torah.

Doubts About the Oral Torah

When the *yetzer hara* despairs of misleading you regarding the written Law, it will try to raise misgivings about the Oral Torah. It will tell you, that while the mitzvos dictated by reason and those written in the Torah are true, what the Sages said is neither important nor binding. But we know the Oral Torah is indispensable for the proper understanding of all mitzvos, whether they are based on reason or on Scriptural texts. Both types of mitzvos cannot be fulfilled correctly without the Oral Torah. For if there were no Oral Torah to specify quality, time, place, and other details of the logical mitzvos, we could not calculate these things on our own. The same is true of Scriptural mitzvos, we could not understand them without an explanation, as our Sages said, "The Torah is expounded through thirteen rules" (Baraisa deRabbi Yishmael), and, "The transmitted Oral Torah is a protective fence around the Torah" (Avos 3:13).

Another verse proving the need of the Oral Torah is, *If you are unable to reach a decision in a case involving capital punishment . . . You must approach the Levites and kohanim and other members of the supreme court . . . they will declare a legal decision . . . You must do as they tell you (Devarim 17:8-10)*, and, *Any man who rebels and refuses to listen to the kohen . . . must be put to death (ibid. v. 12).* When you grasp the significance of this, your doubts will melt away, and you will appreciate that, regardless whether a mitzvah is based on logic or on a Scriptural passage, it requires the elucidation of the Oral Torah.

Doubt About Reward and Punishment

Next the *yetzer hara* will try to make you doubt the principle of reward and punishment. It will begin by telling you that life is unfair: If there were proper reward and punishment in this world, the wicked would not prosper, and the righteous would not suffer, as we discussed in the fourth gate of this book, [the Gate of Trusting God]. But once reason shows you how Divine justice operates, your doubts will fade away, and you will no longer be confused.

When the *yetzer hara* loses hope of capturing you with these ploys, it resorts to making you doubt reward and punishment in the World to Come. It is able to confuse you because there are very few references to this in the Torah, and even those references are only veiled allusions. But consider all the references in the books of the other prophets, such as, *The soul returns to Hashem who bestowed it (Koheles 12:7)*; *I will grant you strides among the [angels] who stand here (Zechariah 3:7)*, [which the Targum translates as—"You will be granted eternal life among the angels in the afterworld"]; *How abundant is Your goodness that You have stored away for those who fear You (Tehillim 31:20)*; *No eye has ever seen a god—except for You—that acted for those who trust in Him (Yeshayah 64:3)*; *Your righteous deeds will precede you (Isaiah 58:8)*, and many others. [Reflect upon] those verses, along with everything the Sages taught us and on that which you can comprehend with our own intellect; then your mind will be serene, and you will be assured that there is reward and punishment in the World to Come.

The Temptation of Worldly Pleasures

Finally the *yetzer hara* tries to make you lazy in your service to God, and keep you busy with worldly things such as, food, drink, dress, travel, and the enjoyment of various physical pleasures. If you listen when it tells you to take pleasure from necessary foods, it will then make luxuries that are less important than food look attractive to you. It will whet your appetite for merriment and amusement, make you envy people in power and their underlings, and make you want to act like them, following their life style and trends of enjoyment. When the *yetzer hara* sees that you are willing and eager to act like that, it says:

"Gird your loins, you fool, and bare your arm, you ignoramus. Go all out to serve this world and its people; maybe you will get some of the things you want. Don't do anything for the next world unless it helps you in this world and makes you popular with people and leaders, with the powers that be, down to plain folks.

"Study only that which will gain you the respect of your contemporaries and will make you popular with the rich and important people, such as: the arts of linguistics, public speaking, grammar, poetry, charming riddles, interesting parables, and striking metaphors. Always try to be in the company of cultured people, and learn how to converse with all classes of people. Never be quiet, for if you are, people will think you are an idiot and a fool. Stay away from all studies which require hard work and are of small benefit."

But the *yetzer hara* will be demolished if from the very start you do not allow your cravings to gain a foothold, and you do not satisfy your desires and chase after luxuries. Tell the *yetzer hara* that you do not need luxuries. You have enough trouble just earning a living, and should God grant you extra income without having to put in additional effort, you would spend it on proper and worthy causes. If He does not [grant you extra income], you will make do with the basic necessities and need nothing else. For if you bow to the *yetzer hara*, you will gradually slide down to the point where you will be ruined in this world and the World to Come.

How the *Yetzer Hara* Entices the Learned

The above mentioned examples of the *yetzer hara*'s methods deal only with its initial approach in which the *yetzer hara* tries to create doubt in the mind of an uneducated person. But if you are knowledgeable about God and His Torah, the *yetzer hara* tries to undermine your faith and befog your knowledge by offering sophistries from logic and the Written and the Oral Torah. These amazing pseudo proofs, seem convincing at first glance, but on closer examination, turn out to be based on false premises.

If you think clearly, you will catch the fallacies in the *yetzer hara*'s proofs and arguments. The truth will become apparent and you will see things for what they are. Your wisdom will be freed from doubt, and your actions will be saved from confusion.

The less knowledgeable you are, however, the more alluring is the *yetzer hara*, and the more easily will it subdue you and control you—inside and out—by challenging you with logical arguments, and feeding you convincing pseudo proofs that dupe you. When the *yetzer hara* finally overwhelms and controls you with the help of your intellect [which swallowed its lies], it will let you down, step by step, from a level that is close to the truth, where falsehood is concealed, to a level where all truth is hidden—the level of absolute falsehood. It will uproot you from this world and make you lose all reward in the World to Come. It will make your wisdom work against you, and your intellect cause your ruin. As it says, *Woe to those who are wise in their own eyes, and in their own view, understanding (Yeshayah 5:21)*, *They have rejected the word of Hashem, so what wisdom is there in them? (Yirmeyah 8:9)*, and, *For the ways of Hashem are straight; the righteous walk in them, and sinners will stumble over them (Hoshea 14:10)*.

Wisdom, when used correctly, can cure any disease [of the soul and the heart], but when used incorrectly [to find proofs for the temptations of the *yetzer hara*,] becomes a pervasive incurable disease. In that way the Torah is compared to fire,—as it says, *Behold, My word is like fire (Yirmeyah 23:29)*. It will light up the eyes of he who wishes to fulfill G-d will, as it says, *God's commandments are clear, making the eyes light up (Tehillim 19:9)*, and *Your word is a lamp for my feet, and a light for my path (ibid. 119:105)*. But it consumes those who stray from its path, as it says, *For with fire Hashem will judge (Yeshayah 66:16)*, *He will rain down coals upon the wicked (Tehillim 11:6)*, [When the wicked people scorned Yirmeyah because he reprimanded them, he said,] *I will not mention Him, and not speak in His name any more, but His word would be like a burning fire in my heart (Yirmeyah 20:9)*.

Be careful not to stray from the path of your forefathers and the early Sages by taking your own advice, and making your own deductions. Don't doubt your forefathers' traditions about what is best for you, and don't contradict the advice they gave you. They have already considered every idea and its implications.

If you think that your thoughts are correct, it may be because you fail to realize the harm that follows in their wake. In your shortsightedness you see only the positive aspects, overlooking the negative angles. As the wise King Solomon said, *Do not move back the long-standing boundary marker that your forefathers established, Hear, my child, the discipline of your father (Mishlei 1:8)*. He described a person who has contempt for his forefathers and abandons their ways, *A generation that is pure in its own eyes, and does not cleanse itself of its filth (ibid. 30:12)*, *A generation that curses its father and does not bless its mother (ibid. v. 11)*, *The eye that mocks a father (ibid. 30:17)*.

Going Beyond the Letter of the Law

[Although you should adhere strongly to the ways and ideas of your forefathers], if, having fulfilled all the required mitzvos, you take upon yourself additional voluntary stringencies, out of pure love of piety, because they make sense to you, and because you are not motivated by selfish interests, that is a good thing. You will be rewarded for it, and you will be acting in accordance with the teaching of the early Sages who said, "Make a fence for the Torah" (Avos 1:1); and, "Why was Jerusalem destroyed? Because they based their actions strictly on the letter of the law, and did not go beyond the requirements of the law" (Bava Metzia 30b). They further said, "Rav Huna said: Whoever occupies himself only with the study of Torah [neglecting to do acts of kindness] is as though he has no God, for it says, '*Many days passed by for Israel without a true God*'" *(2 Divrei Hayamim 15:3)*—i.e. Without both Torah and acts of kindness, a person is without a true God (Avodah Zarah 17b). In conclusion, a devout man once said, "If you don't do more than you have to do, you haven't done enough, but the optional is acceptable only if you have already fulfilled the essential."

The Sages permitted us—even compelled us—to go beyond the minimum requirement of the law. They said, for example, "We should add from the profane to the sacred" (Yoma 81b). They added fasts, extra prayers, additional charities, and told us to avoid overeating permitted lavish foods. They warned us not to take an oath in God's name even for the truth, not to talk too much, even the truth, not to discuss other people's activities even if we don't criticize them, not to praise someone else excessively even if he deserves to be praised, [because too much praise leads to disparagement], not to condemn people who are lax in their observance even if they deserved it, and other teachings like that.

The Wiles of the *Yetzer Hara*

At this point it is worthwhile to illustrate other temptations the *yetzer hara* uses, so that you will be on guard against them. Every precious thing in the world is delicate and can be damaged. Only if you are aware of its frailties, can you be alert to protect it. But if you know only the good side of something and are blind to its weaknesses, you are bound to damage it.

A pious man once instructed his students, "First learn about evil, to stay away from it; then learn about good and do it. As it says, "*Plow for yourself a furrow, and do not sow upon the thorn-bushes" (Yirmeyah 4:3)*. [In other words: First you must uproot the weeds of evil, then you can plant the seeds of good].

Rabbi Yochanan ben Zakkai said concerning the use of false weights and measures, "Woe is me if I speak about it, woe is me if I don't. If I speak about it, dishonest people will learn from me how to cheat; and if I don't speak about it, cheaters will think the Sages are not aware of what they are doing" (Bava Basra 89b). The Gemara then asks: "Did he or did he not speak about it?" The Gemara answers: "He did speak about it, and based his action on the following verse, '*For the ways of Hashem are straight; the righteous walk in them, and sinners will stumble over them' (Hoshea 14:10)*."

Enticements of the *Yetzer Hara*

If the *yetzer hara* has thus far been unsuccessful in raising doubts in your mind, it will offer arguments to undermine your beliefs. If you are wise to its tricks and weak arguments it will not be able to disprove what you know to be true and incontestable. It will then beguile you and make you stray by telling you, "I am so pleased with your conduct, your strong faith, and your sincere devotion to God. You have reached a level of piety not attained by anyone else in your generation. You have done more than enough to show your gratitude to God for His kindnesses and favors.

"The time has come for you to fulfill your worldly obligations and find favor with your fellow man. You know that they can help you or harm you, and that it is to your advantage to be well-liked by people. It is a great disadvantage to be disliked by people. So try to please them and find favor with them, for didn't our Sages said, 'If you are well-liked by your fellowmen, you are well-liked by the Omnipresent' (Avos 3:10)."

You should reply, "What good will it do me to ingratiate myself with someone as weak as myself, who can do nothing to help or harm me, as it says, *'O, cease to glorify man, who has only a breath in his nostrils, for by what does he merit esteem?' (Yeshayah 2:22).*

"And assuming you are right, and I do have an obligation to find favor in the eyes of people, how could I possibly please everyone in my generation? I cannot even please everyone in my household, much less other people!

"The Sages did not mean to require us to try to please everyone. Rather they meant, if a person is admired and praised by young and old alike, and everyone is delighted with what he is doing, that is a clear indication that God has instilled a love for him in people's hearts and given him a good name in people's eyes. As it says "*When Hashem favors a man's ways, even his foes will make peace with him" (Mishlei 16:7)*. God does not do that to those who hate Him. When a person is liked by everyone, it is a proof that the Creator is pleased with him. Our Sages were in no way recommending that a pious person try to win the praise of others for his service to God; such behavior does not befit a righteous person."

Watch out for this and other temptations of the *yetzer hara*, for it always tries to lead you in its direction, to trap you in the net of hypocrisy. When it praises you, answer it like this, "You rave over the fact that I am aware of my obligations toward God. On the contrary, this gives God reason to find fault with me, since my actions fall short of what I know I should do. And even if I did as much as I know I should, would that be enough to thank the Creator for the smallest of the favors He bestows on me? After all, what is my lifespan compared to the existence of the universe? And even that length of time would not be enough to recount all the favors God has bestowed on me. So how can I possibly repay God for what I owe for them? For it says, '*All flesh is like grass, and all its kindness is like a blossom in the field' (Yeshayah 40:6)*, and as our Sages said, 'If I am not for myself, who will be for me? And if I am for myself, what am I?[1] And if not now, when?' (Avos 1:14)."

The *Yetzer Hara* Uses Flattery

When the *yetzer hara* gives up hope of alluring you [to do things to ingratiate yourself with people], it will try to entice you with [your innate] love of praise and reputation in this world. It will tell you, "I am pleased with your service to God, with your strong faith in Him, with your reliance on Him in whatever you do, and your firm belief that no one except God can help you. You really trust God wholeheartedly!

"It is not right for you to hide your piety from others. Now that you have mastered yourself and controlled your desires, you must show people what you are doing and lay bare your pure heart. This will earn you respect and win you fame and popularity. As it says, "*In My house and within My walls I will give them a place of honor*

---

[1] Even if I fulfill the mitzvos, I do not do even a small fraction of what I am required to do (Rashi, Rabbeinu Yonah).

and renown which is better than sons and daughters (Isaiah 56:5), and, [like Hashem said to David through Nathan,] "*I gave you great renown, like the renown of the great men of the world*" (*2 Shmuel 7:9*). Besides, people will learn from your actions, and you will be rewarded for this. Don't hide the things you do, except when it is impossible to reveal them. You will have honor and a good name in this world and a rich reward in the World to Come."

Your answer should be, "What good will praise or a good reputation do me when I know how negligent I have been in fulfilling my duties to the Creator? What enjoyment can I derive from the honor and respect people accord me, when they can neither help me nor protect me from harm? In this respect, are they any different than plants or dumb animals? Besides—I may not achieve honor and a good reputation if I serve God with these intentions; people may take me for a hypocrite, and instead of admiring me they will treat me with disdain. That being so, I would lose either way: on the one hand I would have wasted my actions because I intended to do them for selfish reasons, and will not be rewarded in the World to Come. Nor I will I attain the honor and popularity I hoped to gain in this world."

[Once, a king was listening to the reading of the Torah. His displeasure was noticeable.] He was asked, "Why did you not like the Torah reading of so-and-so? Don't you agree that he has a pleasant voice and is so meticulous in chanting the cantillations?" Replied the king, "How can I enjoy his reading when he is doing it only to please me and find favor in my eyes? If he read it to please the Creator I would enjoy it." In the same vein we tell *chazzanim* who chant new liturgical hymns in order to please the congregation but do not think about God, that such prayers and hymns are not acceptable to God.

Furthermore tell the *yetzer hara*: "Even if I receive honor in this world for my actions, I am afraid that thereby I will lose my reward in the World to Come, because I will have acquired it prematurely in this world."

To bring home this point a story is told about a pious man who went to the marketplace to buy something. He entered a store and a neighbor said to the storekeeper, "Give him a good price and make him happy, because he is a God-fearing and learned man." The pious man said, "I don't want your preferential treatment. I came here to buy something with my money, not with my Torah knowledge." He refused to buy the article from him and went to another who did not know him.

"The verse you quoted, '*I gave you great renown like the renown of the great men of the world'(2 Shmuel 7:9)*, [does not mean that a person should make an effort to acquire a good name]. Rather, a good name is a gift God bestows on His servants when His wisdom ordains that they are worthy of wealth and respect. As [God said to Shlomo,] '*I also grant you what you did not ask for, both riches and glory all your life' (1 Melachim 3:13)*, and, [regarding the Torah it says,] '*In its right hand is length of days, in its left riches and honor' (Mishlei 3:16)*. Nonetheless the righteous have only one thing in mind in everything they do: to act for the sake of the Creator, Who bestows favors on whichever of His servants He pleases—sometimes to believers and at times even to non-believers, as His wisdom ordains. As it says, '*Wealth and honor are Yours to dispense' (1 Divrei Hayamim 29:12)*."

[Tell the *yetzer hara*:] "How great is this world anyway, even if my fame spread all over? And how long is the history of the world, even if during my lifetime I became world-famous? Surely it does not pay to invest a great deal of effort to gain prominence; at best my name would become known to only a small part of the world, and only for a short time, after which it would pass from the scene and be utterly forgotten. As it says, "*Common people are but vanity! Distinguished people are but deceit! Placed on a scale all together, they weigh even less than a breath" (Tehillim 62:10)*, "*His breath departs; he returns to the earth" (ibid. 146:4)*, and, "*There is no recollection of the former ones" (Koheles 1:11)*. Any effort I make to gain fame would be an out-and-out degradation and an appalling error on my part."

The story is told that one pious man asked another, "Do you possess serenity?"

"What do you mean," the other asked.

"Does praise and insult leave you indifferent?"
"No."
"Then you did not reach the level of piety."
Do your best to reach this lofty level for it is the highest form of piety and the most sublime quality attainable.

The *Yetzer Hara* Tries to Distract You During Prayer

When the *yetzer hara* despairs of prevailing upon you [to seek glory through your good deeds], it tries to spoil them by making you think of mundane affairs while in the service of the Creator. These are thoughts both about people, and your desires. By dwelling on these, you forget your destiny. When you are engrossed in things that will earn you a place in the World to Come, such as prescribed or optional prayer, studying the Torah or other books on faith and ethics, the *yetzer hara* will try to distract you with worldly matters like buying and selling, profits and losses. While you are involved in serving the Creator, it will say to you "Use this time, because all the rest of the time you are busy with your business. Now is the time to take stock with your partner and figure out how much you own and how much you owe, how much of your debts have been collected and how much is still outstanding. Now you have a chance to think which business opportunities to take and which to avoid, to reflect on your profitable and unprofitable deals. If you are involved in a lawsuit, this is the time to review all your opponent's arguments and your counterclaims; think of ways to outsmart him and win the case."

Whether you have cash, livestock or a field that needs to be planted, whether you work for government officials or for private individuals, whether you owe money and cannot pay your debts, or whether you have friends you are concerned about, the *yetzer hara* will call one of these things to mind while you are serving God, in order to disturb you and make your service worthless. You will end up serving God mechanically, with your mind and feelings elsewhere.

Perhaps the *yetzer hara* will suggest riddles and bewildering brain-twisters to you during your service to God. If you play dice, chess or the like, you will think of moves to make and strategies to use for winning. If you are a Torah scholar or thinker, the *yetzer hara* will suggest knotty problems concerning the subject you are studying, and will pester you with questions and answers, contradictions and solutions. It may call your attention to a point you overlooked, or to the fact that you have so much more to learn. In this way the *yetzer hara* draws you away from serving God, and does more harm than good.

You may serve God while your mind is involved with mundane matter from beginning to end. Your lips ask God for forgiveness, while your mind is rebelling against Him. You implore Him with your limbs while ignoring Him with your heart. It says about this, "Such a plea for forgiveness requires a plea for forgiveness." This is the underlying thought of the verse, "*With their mouths and their lips they honored Me, but they kept their heart far from Me*" *(Yeshayah 29:13)*, and, "*Yet they deceived Him with their speech, lied to Him with their tongues. Their hearts were not constant toward Him*" *(Tehillim 78:36,37)*.

Wake up from your stupor and say, "How can I behave toward God in a way I would never behave toward a person. Were I to ask someone a favor, mouthing words absentmindedly, he would certainly turn me down.

"All the more would he turn me down if he knew I was thinking about things that enrage him. He would surely hate me, and furthermore he would be justified in denying me the favor. I would act similarly if someone asked a favor of me and I knew his evil thoughts, as the Creator knows my thoughts. This being so, how can I not be ashamed before my Creator, [Who knows what I am thinking of during prayer], if I act toward Him in a way I would not want a person to act towards me. As it says, '*They do not feel shame, and they cannot be made to blush*' *(Yirmeyah 6:15)*."

If you come to this realization you will quell the *yetzer hara*.

The *Yetzer Hara* Says: Hide Your Good Deeds

When the *yetzer hara* despairs of seducing you this way, [it puts on the mantle of moralist] and tells you to abandon your hypocritical ways. It says, "You will never serve God wholeheartedly unless you stay away from hypocrisy completely. The way to stop serving G-d for praise is to hide your good deeds and pretend to be the opposite of what you really are. Cut your prayers short and don't show eagerness and fervor. Study in isolation, so that no one but the Creator knows about it.

"Don't let anyone find out about your good qualities. Act listless in your service to God, so that you don't acquire a good name and thereby lose your reward [in the World to Come]. Do not encourage people to do the right thing or warn them against wrong. Don't advertise how much you know, and don't teach anyone. Don't let your fear of God nor your service to Him be known, so that people do not respect you.

"The best way to hide your exemplary conduct is to become friendly with all kinds of people, to take on their way of life and adopt the frivolous and obscene expressions they use. Don't refrain from lying and swearing. Join with them when they eat, drink and converse. Talk banalities, tell jokes, and engage in talebearing and gossiping. In other words, do all you can to avoid being labelled a saintly person."

If you follow the *yetzer hara's* advice, you will be cheated out of your faith without noticing it. Instead, you should say, "[You say you have come to subdue my enemies, but instead] you are helping them by fighting against me, shrewdly sapping my strength and hastening my downfall. Why should I jump from a small fire into a large one? We avoid fame and glory because we do not serve God in order to ingratiate ourselves to others—yet you are asking me to ingratiate myself to them by abandoning the service of God.

"Those activities that can be performed and completed without anyone knowing should be kept hidden. But just to avoid the attention of people, I will not turn my back on mitzvos that cannot be done privately, such as communal prayer, urging people to do right or to abstain from evil, learning Torah and practicing kindness. Rather, I will do them for the sake of Heaven. My reward will not be reduced if people praise me, because I did not do these mitzvos for praise".

If you do something openly and want to make sure your motives were pure, ask yourself these questions: One; From whom did you expect reward? If you expected it from God, your motives were pure, but if you expected respect and admiration from others, your motives were not pure. Two; would you have done it exactly the same way if you were alone? If you answer in the affirmative, your action was done for the sake of God. Keep on doing it! But if you would have done less, stop doing it until you feel that you have cleansed your heart from ulterior motives and will act for the sake of Heaven. Then you will defeat your *yetzer hara.*

Other Cunning Ploys of the *Yetzer Hara*

If you do not listen to this ploy, the *yetzer hara* will trick you concerning reward and punishment in this world and in the World to Come. It will say to you, "You are one of the Creator's righteous men, one of his treasured individuals. A person like you deserves to be rewarded in this world as well as in the hereafter. Serve God in order to earn this reward; visualize this reward and make it your goal, and you will be able to serve God with ecstatic happiness and joy. As David put it, '*Light is sown for the righteous, joy for the upright' (Tehillim 97:11).*"

By listening to this advice, the *yetzer hara* will bring you to dual worship; you will be serving God and yourself. You will be interested in your own comfort and pleasure and in avoiding worry and tension. If not for the expected reward, you would ignore all favors God constantly bestows on you, paying no attention to your obligations to serve Him in return for them. Furthermore, you would not be serving God because of His greatness, might, and the manifestations of His wisdom. As our Sages said, "Don't be like servants who serve their master for the sake of receiving a reward; instead be like servants who serve their master not for the sake of receiving a reward" (Avos 1:3).

When the *yetzer hara* gives up hope of persuading you with the above argument, it will toss you into a sea of doubts, questioning the seeming contradiction between Divine foreknowledge and the principle of free of will. When you are lax in your observance and transgress, it will try to prove to you that a person's actions are predetermined [by God's foreknowledge], citing convincing arguments from Scripture and the words of the Sages. It will tell you, "If God really wanted you to serve Him, He would force you and prod you. Whatever He decrees happens. How could you possibly go against His directives or resist His judgments? You can only do what you were destined to do, for control is in the Creator's hand, as it says, '*It is I, God, Who made everything*' *(Yeshayah 44:24)*."

But when the *yetzer hara* sees you involved in mundane matters, it will say, "Beware of laziness, and don't depend on anyone but yourself, because success and failure are in your hands. Do your best to get all you want of worldly pleasure, and avoid hardship at all cost. For the wise King Shlomo said, "*Thorns and snares are in the path of the crooked; he who values his life will keep far from them*" *(Mishlei 22:5)*; "*A man's folly subverts his way, and his heart rages against God*" *(ibid. 19:3)*; "*You brought this on yourselves*" *(Malachi 1:9)*.

The *yetzer hara* contradicts himself: Sometimes it argues that you are acting under duress, that everything you do is predestined by the Creator, and at times it presents the opposite view, that you have a free will. It tailors its arguments according to what will entice you to sin and weaken your faith.

Take to heart what our Sages said, *"Everything is in the hands of Heaven, except the fear of Heaven" (Berachos 33b)*, and then you will be fervent in observing the Torah. You will be convinced that one's own actions determine one's reward or punishment, as it says, "*For He repays man according to his actions, and provides for him according to his conduct*" *(Iyov 34:11)*. But you will trust God in worldly matters, knowing that all your ups and downs are ordained by God, as it says, *"Cast your burden on God" (Tehillim 55:23).*

The *Yetzer Hara* Recommends Procrastination

When the *yetzer hara* despairs of tempting you with this approach, it tries to tell you, "Put off your service of God's until later. By serving God properly only one day before you die, you will receive eternal reward and be freed from punishment. After all, you know how to repent. The Creator will accept your repentance as long as you return to Him sincerely."

You should answer as follows, "How can I wait until the day I die, when I do not know when that day will come? Were I to follow your advice, I would be like the servant who was sure his master the king would never fire him. He spent his days indulging in worldly pleasures, thinking to do his work later. When the king asked for a progress report about his work, he had no defense to offer for his negligence. He was dismissed from the king's service and expelled from the kingdom. Since he had not saved money or acquired property while he had the opportunity, he left the palace penniless and deeply depressed. He remained despondent and downcast until his dying day."

When the *yetzer hara* gives up hope of luring you that way, it tries to lead you astray through pride, arrogance and lack of humility. It will tell you, "With your perfect faith and your exemplary conduct you have reached the pinnacle of piety, a level equal to that of the pious and righteous men of old. You are unique in your generation, matchless among your contemporaries. Now the time has come for you to show your superiority by putting others down and treating them with disdain. Point out their shortcomings, call attention to their bad character, degrade and reprimand them, so that they will feel ashamed, return to God, and regret what they did. You will be following in the footsteps of the prophets, for it says, '*You, son of man! Tell the House of Israel about the Temple, and let them be ashamed of their iniquities' (Yechezkel 43:10).*"

You should answer, "How can I humiliate someone when I don't know their inner perspective on God? On the surface his outlook may seem objectionable, but his inside may not be like his outside. When the prophets castigated the people of their generation, they did so with the approval of the Creator, Who looks into people's hearts and knows their evil frame of mind. But I have neither the wisdom nor the knowledge to read people's hearts and minds.

"It is possible that a person who seems objectionable is much better than he seems; I am just not aware of it. In fact, he may be better than me, for he may be negligent only because he is unaware of his obligations to the Creator, while I know my obligations and still fall short. He defies God inadvertently, out of ignorance, whereas I disobey Him mindfully and intentionally.

"Furthermore, it is possible that his wickedness is public knowledge, and his virtues are hidden, while the reverse is true with me. That being so, he deserves more compassion and forgiveness from God than I do. In fact, just one of his merits outweighs many merits of mine, because no one but the Creator sees them, and no one praises or respects him for them. It is the opposite with me. My good deeds are public knowledge, and since people praise and respect me for them, my reward is reduced.

"The same applies to transgressions. One transgression of mine outweighs many of his, because my transgressions are concealed while his are exposed. Since people denounce him for them, his punishment is reduced.

"My reward in the World to Come will be reduced because of the acclaim I receive for my good deeds, and the punishment for my transgressions will remain intact. By contrast, he will rewarded in the World to Come for his good deeds, while the punishment for his transgressions will be reduced because of the indignities he suffered through them.

"Finally, if I worry about the shortcomings of others and ponder their bad traits, I will not have time to think about my own faults. I am like a sick person whose illness prevents him from minding the illnesses of others, and whose own need for treatment prevents him from looking after the healing of others."

Answer the *yetzer hara* this way and you will crush it.

Affluence and Poverty

If, after all its attempts, the *yetzer hara*'s arrows did not pierce you, it will wait until you have become wealthy or have met with misfortune. When you are successful, it will say, "Your success is the result of your own effort, ingenuity and skill. Keep busy in this area. You will move on to even greater achievements. Enjoy life, because death will call you before long and you will have to descend into the darkness of the grave, where there is no action, movement, pleasure or pain. The *yetzer hara* will quote the words of the wise King Shlomo to prove his point, '*Whatever is in your power to do, do it with all your might; for there is no action, no reckoning, no knowledge, no wisdom in the grave where you are going*' *(Koheles 9:10).*"

When you meet with misfortune, it will show you that the wicked are well off and the nonbelievers are successful, as it says, "*Robbers live untroubled in their tents, and those who provoke God are secure*" *(Iyov 12:6).* It will say, "You suffered this setback because you have faithfully served God and observed His mitzvos. Do not go on like this; it is too much of a burden, and, anyway, you will never be perfect. Give up this piety and you will be as happy as the wicked are. Just look in Scripture,[and you will see that God is very strict with those close to Him. As it says] '*I will be sanctified by those nearest Me*' *(Vayikra 10:3)*, and, '*You alone have I singled out of all the families of the earth, that is why I will call you to account for all your iniquities*' *(Amos 3:2).* There are many such passages."

Dissuade You From Doing Mitzvos

When the *yetzer hara* notices that you plan to do a mitzvah, it will [tell you that it is too difficult for you] and scare you. If you plan to fast, it might say, "Fasting saps your strength, makes you sick, and interferes with your work and your spiritual pursuits." If you plan to get up at night to recite voluntary additional prayers, the *yetzer hara* will try to convince you that sleep is more important. If you intend to give charity, the *yetzer hara* will paint a mental image of poverty.

The same goes for all other mitzvos: the *yetzer hara* will try to discourage you from doing them. On the other hand, if you plan to commit a sin, the *yetzer hara* will make it seem attractive and make you forget the punishment. It will encourage you to sin and develop a fondness for it.

Answer the *yetzer hara* by saying that any pain you have suffered in the past [as result of your service to God] has vanished without a trace, whereas the reward you receive will last forever. When you fast all day and eat at night, you feel as if you never fasted; your strength comes back as soon as you eat, but your reward is put away securely. So too, when you stay awake part of the night and then go to sleep, you will feel robust as if you had slept soundly all night, but the reward for staying awake [and praying] will last forever. As far as giving charity is concerned, I have explained that subject in detail in the Gate of Trusting God.

When it comes to sinning, reflect on how quickly pleasures fade, both the permitted and forbidden. Forbidden pleasure leaves you with nothing but disgrace and punishment in this world and in the next. If you answer back the *yetzer hara* like this, you will conquer it. Be eager to do good and refrain from behaving in a shameful way.

When the *yetzer hara* sees that his efforts are futile, that in spite of his nagging you persist in serving God, it will try to fill your heart with anxiety, to make you regret the good you have done. In this way the Creator will spurn your good deed and deprive you of your reward. Conversely, if you commit a transgression, the *yetzer hara* will try to make you enjoy it, so that you develop an appetite for it and will be eager to repeat it.

If you become aware of its ruses and watch out for the traps it sets for you, with God's help, you will be saved from them. But if you do not become aware of these traps, the *yetzer hara* will cast you down without warning and shoot its arrows at you, as it says, "*Until the arrow pierces his liver he is like a bird rushing into a trap, not knowing his life is at stake*" *(Mishlei 7:23)*.

If you are able to resist these maneuvers, the *yetzer hara* will try to get you into its clutches by making you neglect your Torah studies. It will say to you, "Know as much about the Torah as the prominent people of your generation do, [and they know only the fundamentals of the Jewish faith]. There is no end to the wisdom of the Torah. Your goal should be only the fundamentals of the Jewish faith and the basic principles of the Torah, then study the subjects that are rated highly by people, like poetry, meter, flowery sentence structure, amazing riddles, and popular metaphors.

"Desist studying the works of the Rabbinic Sages and their halachic debates. Don't study philosophical concepts, such as inductive and deductive thinking, logic, cause and effect, or the relationship between physics and metaphysics, for these topics are too profound and subtle for you to understand. Rely on the elementary traditions you received from your parents and teachers, even for things you can figure out yourself, the way you rely on them for things that are beyond your comprehension."

If you don't pay attention to the *yetzer hara* and in fact, increase your Torah studies, it will try to make you jealous of your friends. If they are more learned than you, it will make you find fault with them as if they stole your knowledge and robbed you of your wisdom. If you are wiser than they, the *yetzer hara* will make you look down on them. It will make you so arrogant you will claim to know things you don't know. In your pride you will think that you know everything and don't have to study any more. Even when you do learn, you will think that no one else understands it as well as yourself, and you will be indignant when questions are asked. You will constantly think how great a sage you are. You will try to gain honor by pointing out your friends' ignorance and you will boost your own image at the expense of your colleagues' reputations. You will eventually end up devoid of all the morals our Sages taught about God and His Torah.

When the *yetzer hara* fails to sway you from your belief in God and His Torah, it will try to appeal to you in the area of service to God. When you perform one of God's mitzvos, the *yetzer hara* will exaggerate your fulfillment of that mitzvah and make you proud. It will make you look down on your neighbor's performance of the mitzvos, making it easy for you to despise him, when in fact he may be better than you in the eyes of God.

If one of your friends serves God with more dedication than you, performs mitzvos better than you, and tries to draw closer to God than you, the *yetzer hara* will tell you, "Any serious intent on the part of someone else to serve God makes you look bad. If not for this person, you would be the greatest *tzaddik* of your generation. Stir up people against him, be envious of him and hate him. Try to discover his weaknesses and shortcomings. Make every effort to spread false rumors about him, and if you can spoil his reputation, do so."

You should answer: "How can I despise someone God loves, insult someone the Creator praises? Is it not bad enough that I am too lazy to serve God as well as he, should I also hate him because he serves God? That is not the way to repay the Creator for what I owe Him. In order to show my love of Him, I should love those that love Him. In order to honor Him, I should honor those that honor Him, as it says, [when delineating the virtues of the righteous], *'And he honors those who fear God' (Tehillim 15:4)*. For you know that Miriam [was punished when she spoke disparagingly about Moshe's high level of service] as the Torah relates *'Aharon and Miriam began speaking against Moshe' (Bamidbar 12:1)*, and look what happened to Korach and his party when they were jealous of Moshe and Aharon for having drawn closer to God than they!"

CHAPTER SIX

The Obligation to Guard and Control Your Thoughts

Make it a point to guard your thoughts carefully, for your thoughts determine whether your actions are correct or not. As it says, "*More than all that you guard, guard your mind, for it is the source of life*" *(Mishlei 4:23)*, and it says in the Torah, "*For the inclination of man's heart is evil from his youth*" *(Bereishis 8:21)*, and, "*I know their inclinations*" *(Devarim 31:21)*, and, "*For God searches all minds and discerns the design of every thought*" *(1 Divrei Hayamim 28:9)*, and, "*It is something that is very close to you. It is in your mouth and in your heart, so that you can keep it*" *(Devarim 30:14)*, and, "*What does God want of you? Only that you remain in awe of God your Lord*" *(Devarim 10:12)*,—awe of God can only be in the heart and the mind.

Dear brother, you must try [to use your mind and] dedicate all your actions to the Creator. Thereby your toil will not be in vain and your efforts not wasted, as it says, "*Why do you spend money for what is not bread, your earnings for what does not satisfy?*" *(Yeshayah 55:2)*, [meaning: Why exert yourself on a service that is not for the sake of Heaven and does not attain fulfillment?] [Although] I have compiled for you the major factors that keep you from serving God wholeheartedly, [be aware that] each of these has an almost endless number of subdivisions. You must be on guard with all your faculties, so that your actions will be wholeheartedly dedicated entirely to the Creator's name, and they will be accepted and welcomed by Him wholeheartedly.

When serving God, behave the way you do when you deal with mundane matters. [When buying merchandise], you choose the best quality, and avoid damaged or contaminated goods. If you act this way when it comes to worldly, short-lived concerns, surely this should be your attitude for everlasting concerns which bring you closer to God.

Do your utmost to cleanse your actions [from ulterior motives], even if you will be able to do only a few pure deeds. This is more worthwhile than a lot of impure deeds. A few pure deeds are worth a great deal, whereas many impure deeds amount to very little and in fact, are practically worthless. Surely it is not worthwhile if your good deeds are few in number and impure too.

Don't act like the proverbial bird, that lays its egg and carelessly leaves it to hatch on the warm ground where other animals can destroy it before the chick has a chance to emerge, as it says, "*[The ostrich] leaves her eggs on the ground, letting them warm in the dirt, forgetting they may be crushed underfoot, or trampled by wild beasts*" *(Iyov 39: 13-15)*. In fact, the wise King Solomon praises the creature who is diligent and hard-working. He commands us to study it and learn from it, although it is one of the weakest insects. For he said, *"Go to the ant, you sluggard; study its ways and learn . . . how it lays up its stores during the summer, gathers its food in the harvest"* *(Mishlei 6:6-8)*.

In conclusion, we have mentioned a few of the many things [that deter a person from serving God with pure intent]. Don't think of them as too much, and don't be intimidated by them. Bear in mind, that the more precious something is, the more delicate it is, and the more easily it can be damaged. When you understand this, the importance of this book's contents will be evident to you.

May God in His mercy, include us among those that serve Him wholeheartedly, and who act for the sake of His great name. Amen.

Duties of the Heart

GATE SIX

The Gate of Humility

Our Duty to be Humbly
Submissive to God

INTRODUCTION

Since the previous Gate dealt with one's duty to dedicate his actions to God alone, and since pride of one's dedication to God undermines his actions more swiftly than any other influence and gravely inhibits his deeds, it is most important to follow with a discussion of the character trait that counteracts pride, namely: humble submission.

Furthermore, humble submission is the root of service and the way by which a person can stop feeling superior. [Through submission] he will acknowledge that God alone is the Master of all Creation, as David put it, "*Yours, God, are greatness, might, splendor, triumph and majesty—yes, all that is in heaven and on earth*" *(1 Divrei Hayamim 29:11)*, and, "*For who in the skies can equal God, can compare to God among the divine beings?*" *(Tehillim 89:7)*. Submission keeps you from haughtiness, conceit, arrogance, vanity, domination, high-handedness, the desire for things that are beyond your reach, and similar aspects of pride.

We will explain ten aspects of submission:

ONE: What is humble submission?

TWO: The various types of humility.

THREE: Circumstances that make you humble.

FOUR: When to be humble and submissive.

FIVE: How to become submissive.

SIX: How a humble person conducts himself.

SEVEN: Hallmarks of genuine humility.

EIGHT: Is humility a prerequisite for other good qualities, or can they appear without humility?

NINE: Can a person be proud and humble at the same time?

TEN: The benefits of humility in this world and in the hereafter.

CHAPTER ONE

WHAT IS HUMBLE SUBMISSION?

Submission is the character trait of humility, lowliness and feeling insignificant. It is a character trait of the soul which shows itself through one's actions. One will speak gently and quietly, will remain sweet-tempered even when angered, and will not be vengeful even if he is in a position to retaliate.

The story is told about a [righteous] king who appeared in court when a man who had offended him was sentenced to be flogged. When the whip was brought in, the king [not wanting to act in anger] said, "As God lives, if I were not so angry with you, I would take full revenge on you." He then pardoned him. The king explained his conduct saying, "I do not know of a sin grave enough to spoil my humility and make me take revenge."

CHAPTER TWO

The Various Types of Humility

There are three types of humility. The first is found in many species of animals and in some people. It is passivity in the face of assaults; the victim is capable of deflecting these assaults but submits because he does not know how to avoid them. Simpleminded and unlearned people call this humility, because they don't know their own capabilities. In fact, it is foolishness and lack of assertiveness that blinds the victim and prevents him from seeing what is in his own interest. As it says, "*You have hidden understanding from their minds, therefore You will not lift them up*" *(Iyov 17:4)*.

Genuine humility comes about only after you lift your soul above the low level of animals, and above the attributes of vulgar people. This is attained by acquiring wisdom, a noble spirit, and a clear understanding of what good and shameful qualities are. If submissiveness and meekness result from this [elevation above the attributes of vulgar people], then they are admirable qualities; otherwise they are neither good qualities nor virtues of the soul, rather degrading character traits, since this submission is not unlike the servility of animals.

The second kind of humility is subservience one person displays to another, such as a prisoner to his captors or a slave to his master. Another example is the meekness displayed by one who needs something from someone else, such as an employee shows to his employer, the poor show to the wealthy, a student to his teacher, or a debtor—who cannot repay a debt—who humbles and demeans himself before his creditor, as it says, "*The borrower is a slave to the lender" (Mishlei 22:7).*

This kind of humility is also shown by a person who realizes that his moral conduct leaves much to be desired yet does not know what he is supposed to do. When such a person meets the prophet of his generation, or a great rabbi, or someone who can guide him on the right path, he will humble and demean himself before him, as our Sages put it, "To be an attendant of a Torah scholar is greater than learning Torah, for it says, '*Elisha ben Shafat poured water on Elijah's hands' (II Melachim 3:11).* It does not say 'who learned' but 'who poured.' Which teaches us that attending to a Torah scholar is greater than studying Torah" (Berachos 7b). Furthermore it says, "*[Moshe's] servant, the young man Joshua bin Nun, did not leave the tent" (Shemos 33:11).* [The fact that he Joshua is called "his servant" rather than "his student" implies that a servant of a Torah scholar is greater than his student.] The wise King Shlomoh said about the unlearned masses, "*A fool is a slave to the wise" (ibid. 11:29).*

Although this kind of submissiveness is well-suited for a person who needs something from someone else, it does not apply to everyone, and is not appropriate at all times and all places. For submissiveness, humility and meekness are no longer demanded of a prisoner after his release, of a slave when he redeems himself, of a borrower when he repays his debt, of the student when he is no longer with his teacher, and of a poor man when he is not with the rich man [who helped him].

The third kind of humility is submission to the Creator, which is required of all people to pursue all the time, everywhere. This is the humility we will deal with in the present Gate. A person with this submissiveness is characterized in Scripture as: humble, self-deprecating, modest, unassuming, lowly in spirit, having a crushed heart, contrite, tenderhearted, brokenhearted, and lying prostrate.

In this gate, we will only refer to this third and loftiest kind of submission. A person who achieves this, is not far from the road that leads to closeness to God. He will stand before Him and will be accepted favorably by the Creator. For it says, "*God, You will not despise a contrite and crushed heart*" *(Tehillim 51:19)*.

CHAPTER THREE

Circumstances That Make You Humble

There are ten situations that will make an arrogant person act with humility and meekness.

One: When he becomes weak and unable to function normally as a result of sickness, or a frail physical condition, he humbles himself and begs God and his fellow man to help him, as it says, "*He humbled their hearts through suffering*" *(Tehillim 107:12)*.

Two: When he is beset with troubles such as poverty which forces him to appeal to people whom he never had to approach before, he humbles himself before them, approaching them in a submissive frame of mind, as [the prophet said to Eli the kohen], "*And all the survivors of your house shall come and bow low for the sake of a money fee and a loaf of bread, and will say, 'Please, assign me to one of the priestly duties, that I may have a piece of bread to eat'*" *(1 Shmuel 2:36)*.

Three: When someone does a special favor for him out of the goodness of his heart, the beneficiary will be submissive to him, as it says, "*Many court the favor of a great man, and all are the friends of a dispenser of gifts*" *(Mishlei 19:6)*.

Four: When he owes a debt to someone and is unable to repay, he will humble himself before the creditor, as it says, *"If you have no money to pay, why should he take your bedding from beneath you?" (Mishlei 22:27).*

Five: If he is a prisoner of his enemy, he will be subservient to him and surrender himself to him, as it says, "*They afflicted his legs with fetters, his soul came into irons" (Tehillim 105:18)*, and, "*And if they are shackled in fetters, trapped in ropes of affliction" (Iyov 36:8).*

Six: A slave who cannot buy his freedom from his master will be submissive to him, as it says, *"As the eyes of slaves follow their master's hand, as the eyes of a salve-girl follow the hands of her mistress" (Tehillim 123:2).*

Seven: When a person meets with trouble and distress, he will become despondent and his heart will be humbled, as it says, "*Then their unfeeling heart will be humbled" (Vayikra 26:41).*

Eight: When a person does soul-searching and realizes how rebellious he has been against God, Who is deserving of praise because of all the favors He has done. He humbles himself and becomes ashamed before God, as it says, "*My God, I am too ashamed and mortified to lift my face to You" (Ezra 9:6).*

Nine: When the Creator admonishes and puts him to shame for rebelling against Him, he humbles himself and is frightened, as God said about Achav, "*Have you seen how Achav has humbled himself before Me?" (1 Melachim 21:29).*

Ten: When a person feels that death is approaching and his final day is drawing near, he thinks about the terror of death, the final judgment and the summation of his deeds, and he will be humbled. He will regret that his life has come to an end, without an ample store of good deeds to pave the way for him on his journey [to the hereafter], as it says, "*The sinners of Zion are frightened" (Yeshayah 33:14).*

CHAPTER FOUR

When To Be Humble and Submissive

There are seven situations when you are required to be humble and submissive:

One: You should be submissive in your business and social relations with others, as I will explain later (Chap 6:4,5). Scripture describes such a person as one, "*in whose own eyes he is contemptible and repulsive*" *(Tehillim 15:4)*

Two: You should be submissive when you meet sages who are learned in the wisdom of God and His Torah, or pious people who are close to God, as it says, "*Let the righteous one strike me with kindness and rebuke me*" *(Tehillim 141:5)*. And, "*Evildoers will grovel before good people*" *(Mishlei 14:19)*.

Three: When people praise you for your good qualities, be humbled and recall your past sins. God knows them and shows forbearance to give you time to repent. Don't be jubilant because people take you for a righteous man, rather bemoan the fact that the Creator knows your deeds, and you are not fulfilling your obligations to Him and repaying Him for His benevolence. When you reflect on this, you will become submissive to God, as it says, "*I acknowledge my iniquity; I am fearful of my sin*" *(Tehillim 38:19)*.

Four: When people vilify you, humble yourself before the Creator and thank Him for revealing a few of your many shortcomings, to admonish you, and help you repent, as it says, "*He opened their ears to discipline*" *(Iyov 36:10)*.

Five: When the Creator bestows favors on you in this world, humble yourself before Him, because you are heavily indebted to Him for that. Be afraid of this bounty, for when God bestows great wealth on a person, He does so for one of three reasons: either as a favor from the Creator, or as a trial, or as a punishment and a stumbling block.

A sign that the riches were a favor from God, is when the recipient is more preoccupied with fulfilling his duties to the Creator than taking care of his material goods. He serves God more than he did before he acquired wealth. He is not preoccupied with his wealth and doesn't depend on it. Rather he spends it on his obligations to the Creator. Iyov describes his perspective on wealth, how he spent it on his obligations to the Creator, and how little he relied on it, "*If I ever put my trust in gold, or ever said of jewels, 'This is my security!' that would have been a criminal offense, for I would have denied God above*" *(Iyov 31:24,28)*.

A sign that wealth is sent as a trial, is when the recipient is more concerned with protecting his money, making it grow, and insuring it against loss, than with showing his gratitude to the Creator for it. Another sign that God gave one wealth as a test is, if he doesn't derive any benefit or pleasure from it, rather it brings him constant worry about the security of his investments. Such a person will have to give an accounting [in the World to Come] on how he spent his money in this world. About him it says, "*For all his days are painful*" *(Koheles 2:23)*.

A sign that one's wealth is a form of punishment, is when he becomes so involved enjoying it that he fails to fulfill his obligations to the Creator and his fellow man. He forgets to serve God Who bestowed this bounty on him, as it says, "*Yet behold! there is joy and gladness, slaying of cattle and slaughtering of sheep, eating meat and drinking wine, saying, 'Eat and drink, for tomorrow we die'*"

(Yeshayah 22:13), "There are harp, lute, drum, flute and wine, at their drinking parties; but they would not contemplate the deed of God" (ibid. 5:12). This is a punishment disguised as a blessing.

An intelligent person who has good fortune and is successful will humble himself before the Creator, for fear that his prosperity may be a punishment from God, as it says, "*Riches hoarded by their owner to his misfortune*" *(Koheles 5:12).*

Six: You should be submissive before God when you read about reward and punishment, and realize that you have not fulfilled your obligations properly, as it says about King Yoshiayahu, "*It happened that when the king heard the words of the scroll of the Torah, he rent his garments*" *(2 Melachim 22:11).* And God replied, "*Because your heart is soft and you humbled yourself before God . . . I, for My part, have listened*" *(ibid. 22:19).*

Seven: When you are engaged in any act of service, like giving charity, praying, or admonishing someone, don't do it with the slightest taint of pride; instead, you should be humble before God, both externally and internally. Do not consider your act as praiseworthy, rather realize how insignificant it is compared to how much you owe God. You owe Him many times as much as this one act. For it says, "[*You ask,] with what shall I approach God, humble myself before God on high? Would God be pleased with thousands of rams, with myriads of streams of oil? He has told you, O man, what is good! What does God require of you but to do justice, to love kindness and to walk humbly with your God*" *(Michah 6:6-8).*

CHAPTER FIVE

HOW TO BECOME SUBMISSIVE

The easiest way for a person to become submissive is to keep in mind the following seven things:

ONE: He should remember that his existence began with a drop of fetid, decomposing semen and blood. It was nourished by unclean blood in the mother's womb and then emerged as a frail body with delicate limbs. He passed from one stage to the next until he reached maturity. Eventually he reaches old age and departs from the scene. As one sage said, "I am amazed how a person who has twice passed through the channel reserved for the passage of urine and blood can be arrogant and proud."

If he reflects on this and other aspects of the human condition, he will surely feel submissive, as David said, "*God, what is man that You recognize him; the son of a frail human that You reckon with him?" (Tehillim 144:3)*, and, "*A man, born of woman" (Iyov 14:1), "But I am a worm and not a man" (Tehillim 22:7)*, and, "*How much more so man, who is like a maggot, and a mortal who is like a worm" (ibid. 25:6).*

TWO: He should think of the hardships he has to go through in this world, like hunger, thirst, severe cold, scorching heat, disease, trouble and anxiety from which death is the only release. Once he recognizes his vulnerability and his inability to escape these difficulties he realizes that he is actually a prisoner. He will humble himself like a prisoner in a dungeon who cannot be freed without his master's consent. In this context David said, "*Let the groan of the prisoner come before You" (Tehillim 79:11), "Release my soul from confinement" (ibid. 142:8).*

THREE: A person should think about his mortality; death may come at any minute, at which time all his ambitions are cut short. He must leave his possessions; they cannot be provisions for his journey [to the hereafter]. When he imagines himself in the grave, how the radiance of his face turns black, how his corpse becomes wormy, decomposed and putrefied, how his handsome appearance is gone and his body becomes foul-smelling as if it never had been washed, cleansed or had a pleasant fragrance; he will become humble and submissive instead of being haughty, conceited, arrogant and self-admiring. As it says, "*Withdraw from man who has breath in his nostrils, for with what is he deemed worthy?" (Yeshayah 2:22)*; "*Common people are but vanity! Distinguished people are but deceit! Were they to be lifted up on the scales, together they would be lighter than vanity" (Tehillim 62:10).*

FOUR: One should realize how much he owes God Who has been so kind to him, and how lax he has been in the performance of *mitzvos*—both those we can and can not understand. When he realizes that he will have no excuses to offer and how remorseful he will be on the day of final reckoning, he will become submissive and dispirited, as it says, "*For behold, the day [of Final Judgement] is coming, burning like an oven, when all the wicked people and all the evildoers will be like straw" (Malachi 3:19); "Who can bear the day of His coming?" (ibid. 3:2).*

FIVE: You will become submissive when you contemplate the greatness and awesome strength of the Creator Who scrutinizes your surface appearance and inner essence. You can gain a deeper understanding of God's exalted power by reflecting on the stories our Rabbis told about [the amazing powers] of earlier tzaddikim. For example, Rav Sheshes stared at a person [who offended him] and that person turned into a heap of bones (Berachos 58a); and when Yonasan ben Uziel was expounding the Torah, any bird that flew overhead was burned instantly (Sukkah 28a). They tell us that the prophets, who were even greater than the Tannaim and Amoraim became faint when they encountered angels, and prostrated themselves before them, as it is told of Daniel, Yehoshua and others like them. Further, we find in the books of the Prophets that the angels prostrate themselves before the Creator, as it says, "*The heavenly legion bows to You*" *(Nechemiah 9:6)*, and, "*He cannot have faith even in His servants and finds fault with His angels*" *(Iyov 4:18); "In His Temple all will proclaim, 'Glory!'" (Tehillim 29:9)*, and, "*One would call to another and say, 'Holy, holy, holy is Hashem, Master of Legions; the whole world is filled with His glory'" (Yeshayah 6:3).*

A perceptive person does not need to envision God's greatness this way. Think of the ways God manifests Himself in creation—in the sun, the moon, the stars, outer space, the earth and all that is on it, the minerals, plants, and animals—and that will make you appreciate God's exaltedness and power, as it says, "*How great are Your deeds, Hashem; exceedingly profound are Your thoughts. A boor cannot know, nor can a fool understand this" (Tehillim 92:6,7); "All the nations are like nothing before Him" (Yeshayah 40:17); "All the inhabitants of the earth are reckoned as nothing" (Daniel 4:32).*

When you think how insignificant you are in comparison to the population of the world, and similarly of mankind in comparison with the earth, of the earth as compared to the orbit of the moon, and of the moon's orbit as compared to the outer orbit, you realize that the entire universe is like nothing in comparison with the Creator. You will then humble yourself and be submissive to God, as it says, "*What is frail man that You should remember him, and the son of mortal man that You should be mindful of him?" (Tehillim 8:5).*

Six: You will become submissive when you read the books of the prophets, and note the severe punishment God metes out to the arrogant and haughty, and, in contrast, God's powerful providence over the humble and the meek.

About pride it says, "*Humankind's haughty eyes will be brought low, and men's arrogance will be humbled, and Hashem alone will be exalted on that day. For Hashem, Master of Legions, has a day [of retribution] against every proud and arrogant person and against every exalted person—and he will be brought low*" (*Yeshayah 2:11,12*). Speaking about both the proud and the humble it says, "*Hashem encourages the humble; he lowers the wicked down to the ground*" (*Tehillim 147:6*), "*For, though Hashem is exalted, He notes the lowly; and the High One makes Himself known from afar*" (*ibid. 138:6*). And of those who are submissive it says, "*But the humble shall inherit the earth*" (*ibid. 37:11*); "*Because Hashem has anointed me to bring tidings to the humble*" (*Yeshayah 61:1*); "*For thus said the exalted and uplifted One, Who abides forever and Whose name is holy: I abide in exaltedness and holiness, but I am with the despondent and lowly of spirit*" (*ibid. 57:15*). And it says, "*Pride precedes destruction*" (*Mishlei 16:18*); "*Prior to his destruction a man's heart grows haughty*" (*ibid. 18:12*).

SEVEN: When you notice how things change constantly, how quickly kingdoms and governments are overthrown, how people's circumstances are in constant flux, [changing from poverty to wealth, from sickness to health,] how one nation is wiped out for the benefit of another, and how everything ends in death, as it says, "*Like sheep they are destined for the Lower World*" (*Tehillim 49:15*), you will become submissive. You will not boast about your worldly possessions nor rely on them, as it says, "*Praiseworthy is the man who has made Hashem his trust, and turned not to the arrogant, and to strayers after falsehood*" (*Tehillim 40:5*).

Keep in mind these seven points and you will be submissive, so much so that humility will become second nature to you. When you dedicate yourself to living humbly, you will be protected from the adversities concomitant with arrogance, and from sin. As it says, "*So that the awe of Him shall be upon your faces, so that you will not sin*" (*Shemos 20:17*).

Our Sages said, "Consider three things and you will not come into the grip of sin: Know where you came from, where you are going, and before Whom you are going to give justification and reckoning. You came from a putrid drop; you are going to a place of dust, worms and maggots, and you will have to give justification and reckoning before the King of kings, the Holy One, blessed be He" (Avos 3:1).

CHAPTER SIX

How a Humble Person Should Conduct Himself

There are ten ways a humble person should act:

One: He should learn about God and His gracious attributes, and how He made man superior to other living creatures, as it says, "*You give him dominion over Your handiwork" (Tehillim 8:7)*. Once you recognize the awesome magnificence of God, the greatness of His power and the infinite wisdom of the Creator, you will be humble and submissive before Him, learning from the wise King Shlomoh's instruction, "*Do not glorify yourself in the presence of the king" (Mishlei 25:6)*, much less before the King of kings and the Lord of lords, Who cannot be compared to anyone, as Channah said, "*There is none as holy as Hashem, for there is none beside You" (1 Shmuel 2:2)*.

Two: You should know your duties mandated by the Torah and reason. You should study God's Torah, and gather from it and from logic the details of submissiveness and how to practice it.

Three: You should be forbearing for the sake of the Creator, and look the other way when hateful things are done to you, as it says, "*Have I repaid with evil those who paid me evil? [No,] I rescued my tormentors without expectation of reward" (Tehillim 7:5); Do not say, "As he has done to me, so will I do to him" (Mishlei 24:29)*, and our Sages said (Gittin 36b), "It is said of people who suffer insults but do not insult back, who hear themselves reviled but do not answer, who do mitzvos out of love and rejoice in chastisement, *'And let those who love Him be like the powerfully rising sun' (Shofetim 5:31)."* Such a person is referred to by our Sages as "one who acts with forbearance".

Four: You should act kindly to others, speak well of them and judge them favorably, as it says, "*Even in your thoughts do not curse a king" (Koheles 10:20)*. Never slander them, as it says, "*You dispatched your mouth for evil . . . You sit and speak against your brother, you slander your mother's son" (Tehillim 50:19)*. Forgive people who malign you, even if they do not deserve it. The Torah tells us, "*Miriam and Aharon began speaking against Moshe" (Bamidbar 12:1)*. This is followed by, "*Now Moshe was very humble" (ibid. v. 3)*, to teach us that he forgave them. The wise Shlomoh says, "*Pay no attention to everything people say, for your own conscience knows that many times you yourself disparaged others" (Koheles 7:21,22)*; and our Sages said that Rabbi Eliezer stepped down to the reader's desk and recited twenty-four prayers and was not answered. Rabbi Akiva then went down and exclaimed, "Our Father, our King . . ." and his prayer was answered. A Heavenly Voice explained, "It is not that this one was greater than the other, it is just that this one is forbearing and the other is not" (Taanis 25b).

The story is told that a pious man, accompanied by his students, came upon a dog's carcass that gave off a foul odor. "How terrible this carcass smells!" the students said in disgust. "Look how white its teeth are," the pious man retorted. The students instantly regretted their disparaging remark. If it is wrong to insult a dead dog, surely it is reprehensible to insult a living human being! By the same token, if it is good to praise the teeth of a dead dog, then surely it is our duty to praise an intelligent and perceptive person!

The pious man wanted to train his students not to speak evil, so that [guarding their tongues] would become second nature to them. He also wanted to train them to say good about others, so that this too would become ingrained in their character, as it says, "*whose tongue is not accustomed to slander" (Tehillim 15:3)*. About the opposite it says, "*Your tongue devises treachery, like a sharpened razor that works deceit; you loved evil more than good" (ibid. 52:4,5)*; "*What can you profit, what can you gain, O deceitful tongue?" (ibid. 120:3); "The words of a wise man win favor, but a fool's lips devour him" (Koheles 10:12)*.

Five: Be humble about mundane matters, both public and private, in speech and in deed, when active or at rest. Don't let your inside be unlike your outside; meaning, that which you do when you are alone should not be unlike your public actions. Your actions should be well thought out, correct, balanced, and consistent. They should be done in a spirit of submission to God and to people according to their status and the benefit you have received from them in Torah and worldly affairs. As it says, "*Good is the man who is gracious [to the borrower] and lends; who conducts his affairs with justice" (Tehillim 112:5)*. And our Sages said, "Be of humble spirit before everybody" (Avos 4:10), and, "Be yielding to a superior, pleasant to the young" (Avos 3:12).

Six: Be ambitious regarding matters of the World to Come. Don't be content with just doing mitzvos that happen to come your way; never be satisfied with the mitzvos you have made an effort to fulfill. Underrate your mitzvos, service, abilities and efforts, and aim for a higher spiritual level, as it says about King Yehoshafat, "*His heart was elevated in the ways of Hashem" (2 Divrei Hayamim 17:6)*.

Be dissatisfied with yourself for failing to fulfill your Torah obligations, and pray to God for help to better your service and good deeds, as it says, "*My prayers: May my ways be firmly guided to keep Your statues" (Tehillim 119:5)*.

Seven: For the sake of the Creator be submissive in the company of people and avoid arrogance. When doing things for God, shake off your dignity, whether alone or among people. The Torah tells us that, despite his high office, Aharon was commanded "*to remove the ashes" (Vayikra 6:3)* from the Altar each day, in order to remove arrogance from his heart. Similarly [when the Ark was brought to Jerusalem, King David's wife Michal] "*saw King David leaping* *and dancing before Hashem" (2 Shmuel 6:16)* [disregarding the dignity of his royal office], and, [David said] *"I will speak of Your testimonies before kings, and I will not be ashamed" (Tehillim 119:46).*

EIGHT: Be satisfied with whatever source of income comes your way by downplaying your bodily desires. Train yourself to resist physical temptations to have the freedom to fulfill your obligations to the Creator for the great kindness He has bestowed on you. As David said, "*I will run in the way of Your mitzvos, for it frees my heart [from worrying about mundane concerns]" (ibid. 119:32).*

NINE: Take vengeance against the wicked for the honor of the Creator. Don't let your impulse to forgive people for wrongs done to you, sway you to forgive them for wrongs done against God, His prophets or His pious ones. Do not be lenient with a person who takes advantage of someone else, the way you would when he takes advantage of you. Rather, rescue the oppressed and help restore his property, as it says, "*Administer justice diligently, and save the robbed from the hand of an oppressor" (Yirmeyah 21:12)*, and, "*I smashed the fangs of the wicked" (Iyov 29:17).*

Teach people about the service of God, admonish them and make them feel ashamed [of their wrongdoing]. Urge them to do good, and warn them against evil, by setting an example and by pleading with them as best you can. Be quick to carry out God's judgment on those who deserve it, and don't be submissive at this time. As it says about Pinchas, "*Pinchas arose and executed judgment, and the plague was halted. It was accounted to him as a righteous deed, for all generations, forever" (Tehillim 106:30).*

TEN: Speak sparingly in a low voice and restrain your urge to tell jokes. Do not take oaths even concerning the truth, never tell a lie, don't keep company with playful people, and don't enjoy the worldly pleasures that common people enjoy. Do this in a spirit of humility, rather than out of smugness and haughtiness, as the prophet says, "*I did not sit in the company of revelers and celebrate; because of Your mission I sat alone, for You filled me with [prophecies of] fury" (Yirmeyah 15:17).*

CHAPTER SEVEN

THE HALLMARKS OF HUMILITY

There are five signs by which you can tell whether a person's humility is genuine:

ONE: If a person is furious with someone who humiliated him by word or deed, but out of humility subdues his anger and forgives the offender, though he has the opportunity to take revenge, [that is a sign of true humility].

TWO: If one has lost money or suffered the tragic death of a close relative and he regains his composure despite his inner turmoil, accepting the decree of the Creator and recognizing God's judgment as fair, that is proof of genuine humility and submissiveness to God. As it says about Aharon when Nadav and Avihu died, "*Aharon was silent*" *(Vayikra 10:3)*. And as David said, "*Wait silently for [the salvation of] Hashem, and wait longingly for Him*" *(Tehillim 37:7)*, and, "*Therefore, the prudent man keeps silent at that time*" *(Amos 5:13)*.

THREE: A person is truly submissive if, he loathes the adulation he receives for something good he did, minimizing his good deed as little in light of all he owes God. He says to the one who praises him, "Enough, brother! Compared to my sins, my good deed is no more than a spark of fire in the vastness of the ocean! And even if it did amount to something, how do I know that it was not spoiled by ulterior motives, so that God will reject it. As it says, "*When you* *come to appear before Me . . . Bring no more worthless meal-offerings, incense is offensive to Me" (Yeshayah 1:12).*

Surely he should dismiss unwarranted praise and say, "Brother, it is bad enough that I do not meet my obligations toward God. Do not compound my shortcoming with the sin of accepting praise for something I did not do. I know my failings and transgressions better than you do. As David said, *'For I recognize my transgressions, and my sin is before me always' (Tehillim 51:5)."*

When people mention some wrongdoing on his part, he will not offer excuses and alibis to clear his name but admit it, as Yehudah said [about Tamar], "*She is more innocent than I am" (Bereishis 38:26).* He will not embarrass the person who spread the report, nor deny it, nor hold it against he who revealed his misdeed. Rather he will say, "Brother, the sins you have seen me do are nothing compared to the transgressions you are unaware of, which God has kept hidden. If you knew my failings, you would run from me for fear of being punished by God along with me. As a poet once said, "If the smell of my sins were to reach my neighbors, they would stay far from me." And Iyov said, "*If I ever covered my sins like a common man does" (Iyov 31:33).*

If what was said about him was false, he should say to the person who reported it, "Brother, I do not pride myself in denying what you accuse me of, because the Creator has prevented me from doing it, just as He has helped me with so many things. What is surprising is that He concealed the misdeeds I have actually done, which are much more disgraceful than this accusation. Stop, brother: have pity on your merits, and don't lose them, [for the merits of a slanderer are credited to the one he maligned]." The story is told that a pious man was being maligned. When he found out, he sent a basket of the finest fruit to the person who slandered him. Attached to it was a note that read, "I received a gift of your merits, and I am hereby expressing my gratitude to you." Another pious man said, "On Judgment Day, people will be shown a book listing the good deeds they did on this world. Many people will find in that book numerous mitzvos they never performed. "But I never did that!" they will exclaim. They will be told that these mitzvos were done by someone who slandered them. In the same way, a person who defamed someone will find several mitzvos he performed missing from the book. When he asks for an explanation, he will be told, "You lost them when you spoke against so-and-so." Then there are people who will find offenses they never committed. When they protest, "We never did that!" they will be told, "These were added to your account because you maligned so-and-so." As it says, "*Repay our neighbors sevenfold into their bosom, their disgrace with which they have disgraced You" (Tehillim 79:12)*. The Torah warned us against speaking ill of others, saying, "*Remember what God did to Miriam on your way out of Egypt" (Deuteronomy 24:9)*, [and Miriam had been punished for speaking against Moshe.]

FOUR: If God showers special favors on you and makes you exceptionally wise, understanding, wealthy, or admired in government circles, or similar gifts that people tend to be proud of, yet you remain submissive and become even more humble and meek before God and even more respectful and kind toward others, then you will have laid bare your inner self and shown your submissiveness to be sincere. Avraham was like that, for when God said, "*Shall I hide from Avraham what I am going to do? (Bereishis 18:17)*, Avraham retorted, "*But I am nothing but dust and ashes" (ibid. v. 27)*. Similarly, Moshe and Aharon said, "*What are we?" (Shemos 16:7)*, and David said, "*But I am a worm and not a man" (Tehillim 22:7)*. And the wise King Shlomoh had this to say about the subject, "*If the ruler promotes you to a higher position, don't give up your position [of humbleness]" (Koheles 10:4)*.

FIVE: If a person transgressed—in a situation that he cannot be forced by a human ruler to repent—and voluntarily takes God's judgment upon himself, that is an indication that he is sincere in his submissiveness. As it says, "*We have transgressed against our God and have taken in alien women of the peoples of the land" (Ezra 10:2*), and, "*They gave their hand [in oath] to send away their wives" (ibid. v. 19)*.

Through these and similar signs you can tell if a person is sincere in his submissiveness and if his humility before God stems from inner conviction.

CHAPTER EIGHT

Is Humility a Prerequisite for Other Good Qualities or Can They Appear without Humility

To answer the question, whether you need to be perfect in all other traits before you can attain submissiveness, or whether submissiveness comes before all other qualities, I want to point out the following:

In order to properly serve God, you must not dominate others, declaring God alone to be Master of the universe. You must be subservient to God like a servant is to his master. The concepts of "servant" and "master" are inextricably linked, because one is not a servant unless he has a master, and so too a master must have a servant. So too a person can not be called a buyer unless he purchased an article. Servant and master, buyer and acquisition, are interdependent, you cannot have one without the other. You cannot be a servant of God unless you act like a servant, being submissive and humble before God, without any thoughts of dominance, such as, eminence, glory, haughtiness, bragging, arrogance, etc. As a Sage once said, "Eminence is the Creator's cloak, as David said, '*Hashem is King, He is robed in grandeur*' *(Tehillim 93:1)*. Whoever dares to wear His robe [by acting with grandeur] is comparing himself to God."

You cannot be considered a true believer until you have fulfilled your obligations, as it says, "*surely, obedience is better than bringing an offering"* *(1 Shmuel 15:22)*. You cannot fulfill your obligations unless you resolve to be a servant to God, and you cannot serve God, unless you are subservient to Him, removing all traces of dominance from your heart. This you can do only if you are humble as we explained.

Thus we see that all other good qualities are dependent on submission. It is their root and origin. It is fair to say that a person cannot acquire any other good traits if he is not humble before God, and if he has even the slightest trace of pride. Furthermore, the traits of humility and submission are also the underpinnings of repentance [which is the subject of the next Gate], as it says, "*My people upon whom My Name is proclaimed, humble themselves and pray and seek My presence and repent of their evil ways"* *(2 Divrei Hayamim 7:14)*, and, "*They have humbled themselves; I will not destroy them"* *(ibid. 12:7)*.

CHAPTER NINE

Can a Person Be Proud and Humble at the Same Time?

There are two kinds of pride. One deals with pride of your physical qualities and material possessions. The other involves being proud of your spiritual qualities, your wisdom or the good deeds you perform in the service of the Creator.

Since pride in physical features runs counter to humility, they cannot coexist in the same person. They are mutually exclusive, because pride in physical values is rooted in contempt of the One Who bestows the favor [about which the proud person boasts]. He does not appreciate the gifts he received nor realize how quickly they may be taken from him. He imagines that he achieved it through his own talent and wisdom, as Sancheriv said, "*With the strength of my hand have I accomplished*" *(Yeshayah 10:13)*, and as Nevuchadnetzar said, "*Is this not the great Babylon which I have built up into a royal house with my powerful strength?*" *(Daniel 4:27)*, and as Pharaoh said, "*Mine is my river, and I have made it myself*" *(Yechezkel 29:3)*. You know what happened shortly after they said these things: their kingdoms were laid waste and their monarchies were destroyed.

Spiritual pride falls into two classes, one deplorable, the other commendable. It is deplorable to take pride in one's wisdom and to boast of one's good deeds. As a result of bragging he overrates his good deeds and is content with what he has done, and rests on his laurels. He thinks that the good reputation he has earned is enough. This kind of pride makes him look down on others, and hold the rabbis of his generation in contempt. It makes him take delight in the shortcomings of others. Our Sages describe this kind of person as "One who elevates himself by degrading others" (Yerushalmi, Chagigah 2:1). A person who acts this way can never be humble.

Spiritual pride is admirable when you are proud of your wisdom and good deeds because you acknowledge the favor that God has done you, and you are happy to do good things. Such pride prompts you to learn more and do more good deeds, be humble toward those who are close to God, be happy for your friends and sensitive to their honor; to hide the ignorance of others, praise them, love them, defend them, and never hurt their feelings. It is commendable to take pride in your service, if as a result, your good deeds seem few to you, and you constantly try to do more of them. You become heartbroken when you are unable to learn and do many good deeds. This pride will enable you to humble yourself before one who can help you; and cause you to thank God for granting you noble qualities. This kind of pride does not negate humility. Rather, such pride reinforces and increases your humility, as it says, "*The result of humility is fear of Hashem*" *(Mishlei 22:4)*. Scripture tells us that it was precisely this kind of pride that inspired Yehoshafat, as it says, "*His heart was elevated in the ways of Hashem*" *(2 Divrei Hayamim 17:6)*.

CHAPTER TEN

The Benefits of Humility in This World and in the Hereafter

Submission to God engenders six benefits, three in this world and three in the next.

The following are the benefits of humility that accrue to you in this world:

One: When you are humble, you are happy with your lot. An arrogant and conceited person is dissatisfied even if he owns all the riches in the world. He turns up his nose at everything [because he thinks he deserves more]. But a submissive person doesn't think he is special, therefore whatever he earns is enough for him to live on. Thus, he enjoys peace of mind, being content with the bare minimum.

But the whole world cannot fill a proud person's insatiable appetite. As the wise Shlomoh said, "*A righteous man eats to be satisfied, but the belly of the wicked is always empty*" *(Mishlei 13:25).*

Two: When you are submissive, you accept misfortune [because you think you don't deserve better]. By contrast, an arrogant person lives in constant fear [of bad things that may happen], and he cannot come to terms with disaster, because of his haughtiness and resentment. It says about a person who behaved this way, "*How* *have you fallen from the heavens, O glowing morning star; been cut down to the ground, O conqueror of nations" (Yeshayah 14:12).*

THREE: If you are humble, people like you, and you get along with them and can adapt to their life-style. The story is told of a king who hurried when he walked, [unlike other monarchs who walk at a slow and dignified pace]. He explained, "It is the least pompous way of walking; besides, it gets me faster to where I want to go."

A wise man once was asked how he became the leader of his generation. He replied, "I never met anyone I did not consider my superior in some way. If he was a greater sage, I said: Since he knows more, he is probably more God-fearing than I. If he knew less than me, I said: On the Day of Judgment he will be judged more leniently, because I sinned intentionally whereas he sinned inadvertently. About an older person I said: No doubt he has accumulated more merits than I, because he was born before me. If he were younger, I said: He has committed fewer sins than I. If we were equal in age and wisdom, I said: Probably he is more devoted to God than I; for I know my transgressions, but I do not know if he has committed any. If he was wealthier, I said: He gives charity, and supports the needy better than I. If he was poorer, I said: In all likelihood, he is more humble and, therefore, a better person than I am. With that attitude I never failed to respect people and treat them with deference. As our Sages said, "Judge everyone favorably" (Avos 1:6); "Be exceedingly humble in spirit" (Avos 4:4); "A person should always be as soft as a reed rather than as hard as a cedar," which is why the reed was worthy to be whittled down to a pen for writing Torah scrolls, *tefillin* and *mezuzos*" (Taanis 20b).

The following are three benefits of humility that accrue to you in the World to Come:

ONE: You can acquire wisdom more easily, because you are fascinated by Sages, are submissive to them, and keep company with them, as it says, "*One who keeps company with the wise will grow wise" (Mishlei 13:20)*, and as our Sages said, "Let your house be a meeting place for Sages, sit in the dust of their feet, and drink their words thirstily (Avos 1:4). God will then help you gain wisdom , as it says, "*He leads the humble with justice, and teaches His way to the humble*" *(Tehillim 25:9)*.

A haughty person cannot attain true wisdom and will never arrive at pure understanding because he is too proud to go to Sages and Torah scholars, as it says, "*The wicked man, arrogant as he is, does not seek information*" *(Tehillim 10:4)*.

TWO: A humble person hurries to perform mitzvos eagerly. He does not boast about, nor belittle any of his deeds, as our Sages put it, "Be as scrupulous in performing a 'minor' mitzvah as in a 'major' one" (Avos 2:1). But an arrogant person puts off performing mitzvos. He remains unconcerned until he falls and is degraded. As it says, "*Say to the king and the queen mother, 'Humble yourselves, sit, for your dominions have collapsed, the crown of your glory'*" *(Yirmeyah 13:18)*, and, "*God hates six things . . . haughty eyes. . .*" *(Mishlei 6:16,17)*.

THREE: When you are submissive, God willingly accepts your good deeds, as it says "*The sacrifices God desires are a broken spirit*" *(Tehillim 51:19)*. Your transgressions are quickly forgiven when you repent of them, as it says, "*He who confesses and forsakes [his sins] will be granted mercy*" *(Mishlei 28:13)*; "*When people are downtrodden you would say, 'Arise;' for He saves the humble*" *(Iyov 22:29)*.

SUMMARY

The ten principles of submission set forth in this Gate will shed light on other aspects of this lofty trait that were not mentioned in this Gate.

Remember what I pointed out to you about this quality, keep it in mind all the time, and try to make it your own. Fuse it to your personality, and God will help you with it. Ask Him to give you this quality in order to draw closer to Him and to do His will. Perhaps He will guide you to it and clear the way to Him for you. As the devout people say in the conclusion of the *Shemoneh Esrei*, "My God, guard my tongue from evil and my lips from speaking deceitfully. Let my soul be silent to those who curse me, and let my soul be like dust to everyone" (Berachos 7a). Be careful with your thoughts and vigilant against the temptations of the *yetzer hara* which tries to make you arrogant, proud, haughty, overbearing, highhanded, and hungry for power and publicity. The wise Shlomoh taught us to follow the path of the "golden mean" saying, "*Two things I ask of You; do not deny them to me before I die: Keep vanity and falsehood far from me; give me neither poverty nor wealth, but provide me with my daily bread, lest I be sated and renounce You, and say, 'Who is Hashem?' and lest I become impoverished and steal" (Mishlei 30:7-9)*.

Wake up, brother! Cure yourself from pride. Don't be deterred because most people neglect to cure themselves from this malady. Don't say, "I don't care. What happens to everyone will happen to me." If a blind person had a drug to cure his blindness, he would not be in his right mind if he delayed taking it and said, "Whatever happens to my fellow blind people will happen to me!" Likewise, care for your soul, and work hard for its benefit. Do not neglect doing whatever it takes to help you in this world and in the World to Come, for you may die without attaining the precious traits you strove for and could have had. As the wise Shlomoh said, "*The craving of a lazy person kills him*" *(Mishlei 21:25)*, and, "*I passed by the field of a lazy man, by the vineyard of a man lacking sense. It was all overgrown with thorns, nettles had overgrown its surface; and its stone wall was broken down. I observed and took it to heart; I saw it and learned a lesson*" *(ibid. 24:30)*.

May God, in His mercy and kindness, show me, and you the reader, the way to serve Him. Amen.

Duties of the Heart

Gate Seven

The Gate of Repentance

Our Obligation to Repent
and its Particulars

INTRODUCTION

In the previous Gate, we discussed the trait of humility, which is the root and starting point of repentance. I thought it beneficial to follow with an explanation of the particulars of repentance and how to fulfill it to perfection.

Logic and the Torah dictate that we need to repent. This is because people fall short of fulfilling their duties toward the Creator. Man's personality is a blend of psychological forces, conflicting emotions, and paradoxical character traits. As a result of this inner divergence, his actions are inconsistent and changeable; sometimes he is charming, other times disagreeable; sometimes he is unfair, other times righteous; sometimes good, other times evil. That is why man needs the restraints of the Torah and the guidelines of tradition.

There are many Scriptural verses about this subject, including, "*Every impulse of [man's] innermost thought was only for evil, all day long*" *(Bereishis 6:5)*; *"Let one who is like a wild ass, be reborn as a man!" (ibid. 11:12)*, and "*How can man be considered righteous before God? How can one born of woman be considered pure? Behold! the moon passed by and cast no light; how much more so man, who is like a maggot, and a mortal who is like a worm!" (Iyov 25:4-6).*

Since we are remiss in doing our duty, the Creator graciously and lovingly gave us the ability to correct our mistakes and make up for our lost service to Him, through repentance. He stressed its importance and through His servants, the prophets, assured us [that it would be effective]. He made allowances for our wayward behavior and promised to accept our repentance; to forgive and forget at once, even if we disobeyed Him and violated His covenant for a long time. As is explained in the segment that begins with the words, "*If a wicked person turns back from his wickedness and acts with justice and righteousness, he shall live" (Yechezkel 33:19).*

[Repentance is essential even for the righteous,] for there are two kinds of righteous people: those who have always been free of sin, and those who have sinned and repented. Since most righteous people are *baalei teshuvah* [penitents], the psalmist began with the words, "*Praiseworthy is one whose transgression is forgiven, whose sin is covered over" (Tehillim 32:1)*. The righteous who have always avoided sin are referred to in the next verse, "*Praiseworthy is the man to whom Hashem does not ascribe iniquity, in whose spirit there is no deceit" (ibid.v. 2)*. This category is mentioned last because there are few of them in every generation, as it says, "*If You preserve iniquities, O God, O Lord, who could survive?" (ibid. 130:3); and "For there is no man so wholly righteous on earth that he [always] does good and never sins" (Koheles 7:20)*. "*For there is no man who never sins" (1 Melachim 8:46)*. That is why our Sages began the blessings of the *Shemoneh esrei* with prayers for repentance and forgiveness; "Bring us back to Your Torah" and "Forgive us, our Father, for we have erred."

I will now explain ten aspects of repentance:

ONE: The definition of repentance.

TWO: How many categories of repentance there are.

THREE: What is essential in repentance.

Four: The elements of repentance.

Five: The specific details of repentance.

Six: The motivations for repentance.

Seven: The deterrents to repentance.

Eight: Comparison of one who repented to one who never transgressed.

Nine: Can a sinner repent of every sin?

Ten: Advice for a person who has difficulty repenting of his sins.

CHAPTER ONE

The Definition of Repentance

Repentance is rectifying your service to the Creator, after you sinned against Him, and fulfilling what you failed to do, either because you were ignorant of God and the ways of serving Him, or because your *yetzer hara* overpowered you, or you forgot your duties to God, or you associated with people who tempted you to sin, as the wise Shlomoh said, "*My child, if sinners seduce you, do not be enticed" (MIshlei 1:10)*, and "*Fear Hashem, my child, and the king. Do not mix with inconsistent people" (Mishlei 24:21)*.

There are two ways to neglect your service of the Creator: either by not doing what God commanded you to do, or by doing something He warned you against, intending to rebel against Him. If you neglected to do what you were commanded, you repent by doing the right thing and by carrying out the main points of repentance as I will explain later in this Gate. If you did something the Creator warned against doing, you must never repeat that act, and try to do the opposite, while carrying out the main points of repentance.

This can be compared to someone who became sick due to his diet. He may have not eaten wholesome food or he may have eaten harmful foods. If he became sick because he did not eat wholesome food, then he should begin eating nutritious food. Once he regained his health, he could keep a moderate diet. But if he became sick from eating harmful food, he must stop eating those foods and eat foods that counteract and neutralize the toxic substances he had ingested, until he recovers. When he recovers, he can stop eating these therapeutic foods and begin eating a balanced diet.

In fact, Scripture compares sin to bad food, for it says, "*Every man will die for his own sin, and the man who eats the sour grapes, his own teeth will be set on edge*" (*Yirmeyah 31:29*).

CHAPTER TWO

The Categories of Repentance

There are three kinds of repentance. There is the repentance of the person who usually does not have the opportunity to transgress, but whenever the opportunity presents itself, his *yetzer hara* overpowers him. Each time he commits the sin, he realizes how disgraceful it was and regrets it.

Such a person repents with his mouth but not with his heart; with his words but not with his deeds, and he deserves to be punished by the Creator. Scripture says about such a person, "*Can one steal, murder, and commit adultery and swear falsely and burn incense to the Baal and go after the gods of others that you never knew, and then come and stand before Me in this Temple, upon which My name is proclaimed and say, 'We are saved!'—in order to [continue] committing these abominations?" Has this Temple, upon which My Name is proclaimed become a cave of criminals in your eyes?" (Yirmeyah 7:9,10)*.

A second person repents in his heart and in his deeds; he overcomes his *yetzer hara*, training himself to resist his desires, and he turns away from what his Creator hates. Nevertheless, this person still tends toward things that are against God; deep down he still yearns to sin. He tries to hold sway over his inclination; sometimes it overpowers him, while occasionally he gets the upper hand.

This repentance does not insure forgiveness. He is forgiven only when he stays away from sin altogether, as it says, "*Therefore, through this shall Jacob's iniquity be atoned for, and this shall be the fruit of his sin's removal: When he makes all the altar stones [of idolatry] like ground chalk stones, and Asherah-trees and sun-idols arise no more" (Yeshayah 27:9).*

The third person complies with all the requirements of repentance. His reason prevails over his desires, he regularly does serious soul-searching, he is in awe of his Creator and is contrite in His presence, he takes to heart the gravity of his sins, recognizing the greatness of the One against Whom he rebelled and whose commandments he transgressed, he always has his transgressions before him, and is remorseful about them, until the day he dies. A person like this is worthy to be saved by the Creator [from the punishment for his sins].

CHAPTER THREE

The Essentials of Repentance

Repentance is possible only after you are aware of seven things:

One: You must clearly recognize that you did the deplorable deed. If you doubt whether you did it, or think that perhaps you did it unintentionally or inadvertently, you cannot truly regret having done it or ask to be forgiven for it, as it says, "*For I recognize my transgression, and my sin is before me always*" *(Tehillim 51:5)*.

Two: You must know how reprehensible your deed was. If you are not convinced that your deed was wrong, you will neither regret it nor accept upon yourself the specifics of repentance. You will think of yourself as having done it by mistake, with a valid excuse, as it says, "*Who can discern mistakes? Cleanse me from unperceived faults*" *(Tehillim 19:13)*.

Three: You must understand that you deserve punishment for your deed. If you don't realize this, nothing will prompt you to regret your action. However, if you realize that you will be punished, you will be remorseful and ask for forgiveness from God. As it says, "*For now that I have returned I am filled with remorse, now that I am made aware [of the punishment that awaits me] I slap my thighs [in anguish]*" *(Yirmeyah 31:18)*, and, "*My flesh shuddered from dread of You, and I feared Your judgments*" *(Tehillim 119:120)*.

FOUR: You must be aware that your transgression is recorded in the book of your wrongdoing; it is neither overlooked, forgotten, nor set aside, as it says, *"Is it not revealed with Me, sealed in My treasuries?" (Devarim 32:34)*, and, "*He seals a judgment with the hand of every man, so that all people He has made shall know" (Iyov 37:7).* If a person thinks that his transgressions are unimportant, he will neither regret nor ask forgiveness for them. Since his punishment is delayed, [he thinks it has been canceled], as it says, "*Because the sentence for wrongdoing is not carried out quickly—that is why men are encouraged to do evil" (Koheles 8:11).*

FIVE: You must believe that repentance is the remedy for your disease and through repentance you can correct your errors and recover your losses. If you are not convinced, you will give up hope and you will not ask the Creator for forgiveness for your past misdeeds, as it says, "*Thus have you spoken, saying, 'Since our sins and our iniquities are upon us, and we are wasting away because of them, how can we live?'" (Yechezkel 33:10)*, to which the Creator replied through His prophet, "*As I live!', so says God the Lord, '[I swear] that I do not desire the death of the wicked one, but rather the wicked one's return from his way, that he may live'" (ibid. v. 11).*

SIX: You must give thought to the favors God has shown you, and how you repaid Him with disobedience rather than gratitude. Weigh the punishment you will receive for a transgression against the pleasure you derive from it, and balance the satisfaction you will obtain as reward for your good deed in this world and the next, against the discomfort your good deed entailed. As our Sages said, "Calculate the cost of a mitzvah against its reward, and the reward of a sin against its cost" (Avos 2:1).

SEVEN: You must do your utmost to keep away from your accustomed vice. Resolve in your heart and make up your mind to shake it off, as it says, "*Rend your hearts and not your garments" (Yoel 2:13).*

Once these seven points are firmly fixed in your mind, it is possible for you to repent of your transgressions.

CHAPTER FOUR

The Elements of Repentance

There are four elements to repentance: (1) being remorseful for past sins; (2) abstaining from them; (3) confessing them and asking to be forgiven for them; (4) resolving in heart and mind never to commit them again.

Remorse is a sign that you regard your action as shameful, as it says, "*Whoever knows [that he sinned], let him repent and regret, and it will leave a blessing behind it*" *(Yoel 2:14)*, and about a person who continues to sin it says, "*No man relents of his evil, saying, 'What have I done?'*" *(Yirmeyah 8:6)*.

We see evidence of [the beneficial effects of remorse] in everyday life. If someone wronged his neighbor and then says he is sorry, that is the stimulus for his neighbor to forgive him.

Abandoning sin is proof that you believe in reward and punishment, as it says, "*Let the wicked give up his way, the sinful man his plans; let him turn back to Hashem, and He will pardon him*" *(Yeshayah 55:7)*, but about a person who continues to sin it says, "*I became angry because of his sinful thievery; I struck him. I hid Myself and became angry, because he continued waywardly in the path of his heart*" *(ibid. 57:17)*. We see an example of this in personal relationships: When a person who harmed his neighbor stops wronging him, his neighbor forgives him and wipes the slate clean.

Asking for forgiveness is a sign of submission before God.

Confessing your sin brings about Divine forgiveness, as it says, "*He who confesses and gives up [his sins] will find mercy" (Mishlei 28:13)*, while the opposite behavior is described in the verse, "*Behold, I will bring you to judgment for saying, 'I have not sinned!'" (Yirmeyah 2:35)*, and, "*He who covers up his faults will not succeed" (Mishlei 28:13)*.

Similarly when someone confesses that he wronged his friend, and asks his forgiveness, the neighbor will realize that he is truly remorseful and will pardon him at once.

Resolving not to repeat your wrongful deed shows that you recognize the magnitude and gravity of your offense, as it says, "*If I have done wrong, I will not continue" (Iyov 34:32); "Take words with you and return to Hashem. . . Ashur will not save us; . . . we will no longer say, 'O our gods' to the work of our hands" (Hoshea 14:3)*. Of someone who does the opposite, it says, "*Can a Cushite change his skin color, or a leopard its spots? Just as much can you -in whom evil is ingrained—do good" (Yirmeyah 13:23)*. We notice the same thing in human relations. When one wronged his neighbor then admits it, is remorseful, and resolves never to repeat it, his neighbor will forgive and not punish him.

If one who repents exhibits these four elements of repentance, as well as their particulars which we will discuss later, the Creator will forgive his iniquities and overlook his transgressions.

If he committed a sin about which it says, "*God will not allow him to go unpunished" (Shemos 20:7)*, such as swearing falsely or adultery, the Creator will ease his punishment in this world and show him favor in the World to Come, and he will be accepted in the assembly of the righteous, as it says, "*A redeemer will come to Zion, and to those of Jacob who repent of willful sin" (Yeshayah 59:20); "If you repent, O Israel—the word of Hashem—you will return to Me" (Yirmeyah 4:1)*, and, "*If you repent I will bring you back, let you stand before Me" (ibid. 15:19)*.

CHAPTER FIVE

Specific Details of Repentance

The main elements of repentance comprise a large number of specific details, but I will mention only twenty of them, five for each of the four basic elements. That way, each of the four elements will be outlined completely.

The Particulars of Remorse

There are five details of remorse:

The first: To fear that the Creator's punishment for your sins is fast-approaching. This fear will intensify your regret, as it says, "*Give honor to Hashem your God before it gets dark, and before your feet stub themselves upon the mountains of the night*" (*Yirmeyah 13:16*).

The second: To be humble before God because of your sins, as it says, "*My people, upon whom My Name is proclaimed, humble themselves*" (*2 Divrei Hayamim 7:14*).

The third: To change your mode of clothing and jewelry, showing contrition in the way you speak, eat, and move about, as it says, "*For this don sackcloth, lament and mourn*" (*Yirmeyah 4:8*), and, "*Both man and animal shall cover themselves with sackcloth*" (*Yonah 3:8*).

THE FOURTH: To weep and lament for the sins you committed, as it says, "*My eyes shed streams of water because they did not keep your Torah" (Tehillim 119:136)*, and, "*Between the Hall and the Altar let the Kohanim, the ministers of Hashem, weep" (Yoel 2:17).*

THE FIFTH: To criticize and humiliate yourself for being careless about fulfilling your obligations to the Creator, as it says, "*Rend your hearts and not your garments" (Yoel 2"13).*

THE PARTICULARS OF ABANDONING SIN

There are five parts to abandoning sin.

THE FIRST: To abstain from everything forbidden by God, as it says, "*Despise evil, and love good" (Amos 5:15), "Praiseworthy is the man . . . who guards his hand against doing any evil" (Yeshayah 56:2)*, and, "*Let the wicked one forsake his way" (ibid. 55:7).*

THE SECOND: To forsake permitted things that may lead to forbidden things, for example, to abstain from something when you are doubtful if it is permitted or forbidden. Pious people would abstain from seventy kinds of permitted things, for fear of stumbling into one forbidden thing. Being careful with the precautionary measures the Sages instituted is another example, as it says, "Make a protective fence for the Torah" (Avos 1:1).

THE THIRD: To avoid sin and restrain yourself because of fear of the Creator's punishment, although you have the ability and opportunity to sin, as it says, "*My flesh shuddered from dread of You, and I fear Your judgments" (Tehillim 119:120).*

THE FOURTH: To avoid sinning because you are ashamed before the Creator—not because you fear or are ashamed of others, or want something from them. Do not be like those about whom it says, "*Their fear of Me is like rote learning of human commands" (Yeshayah 29:13)*, or like it says "*Yeho'ash did what was proper in the eyes of Hashem as long as Yehoyada the Kohen was alive and guided him" (2 Melachim 12:3).*

THE FIFTH: To divorce yourself completely from wrongdoing, so that the thought of repeating the offense would be unthinkable, by saying in your heart and in words what the pious Elihu, said, "*If I have done wrong, I will not continue*" *(Iyov 34:32)*.

THE PARTICULARS OF ASKING FORGIVENESS

Asking forgiveness embraces five details.

THE FIRST: To confess that you transgressed and believe that your sins are great, as it says, "*For our sins are great before You*" *(Yeshayah 59:12)*.

THE SECOND: To always remember your transgressions and set them before you, as it says, "*For I recognize my transgressions, and my sin is always before me*" *(Tehillim 51:5)*.

THE THIRD: To fast during the day and pray at night when you are not distracted by worldly concerns, as it says, "*Arise, cry out in the night!*" *(Eichah 2:19)*. With God's help, in future chapters (Tenth Gate, Chap. 6) I will explain the advantages of praying at night.

THE FOURTH: You must implore God, praying to Him constantly, to forgive your transgressions and accept your repentance, as it says, "*I acknowledge my sin to You; I did not cover up my guilt; I resolved, 'I will confess my transgression to Hashem,' and You forgave the guilt of my sin*" *(Tehillim 32:5)*, "*Therefore, let every devout person pray to You in a time when You may be found*" *(ibid. v. 6)*.

THE FIFTH: To warn others not to stumble into sins like your's, frightening them with the punishment in store for sinners and encouraging them to repent of their sins. As it says, "*He who knows [that he sinned] will repent, and God will relent*" *(Yonah 3:9)*, and, "*I will teach transgressors Your ways*" *(Tehillim 51:15)*.

The Particulars of Resolving not to Backslide

The resolve not to backslide also encompasses five details.

The first: To weigh the immediate but short-lived pleasure you derive from the sin against the permanent and pure gratification that is yours in the hereafter, as it says, "*You will see and your heart will exult" (Yeshayah 66:14)*,

Furthermore, weigh the passing discomfort that doing a mitzvah entails, against the never-ending, anguish in the world to come that stems from transgression, as it says, "*And they will go out and see the corpses of the men who rebelled against Me, for their decay will not cease and their fire will not be extinguished" (Yeshayah 66:24); "For behold the day is coming, burning like an oven, when all the wicked people and all the evildoers will be like straw; and that coming day will burn them up . . . But a sun of righteousness will shine for you who fear My name, with healing in its rays" (Malachi 3:19,20)*.

When you take this to heart, you will not revert to your past transgressions.

The second: To think about your day of death, when your Creator will be angry with you for neglecting your duty, as it says, "*Who can bear the day of His coming?" (Malachi 3:2)*. Reflecting upon this, you cannot help but be afraid of His punishment, and you will resolve never to sin, provoking God's anger.

The third: To reflect about the length of time you have turned your back on God, though all that time He has been good to you. As it says, "*For I [God] have always broken your yoke and torn off your straps, and you [Israel] said, 'I will not enter'" (Yirmeyah 2:20)*. In this context, the phrase "*I will not enter*" means: I will not take upon myself to serve You, and I will not enter into your covenant, as if it had said, "I will not pass into the covenant," as in the verse, "*To pass into the covenant with Hashem your God" (Devarim 29:11)*.

The fourth: To return stolen goods, avoid immorality, and refrain from causing injury to anyone, as it says, "*The wicked person returns a pledge, repays for his theft" (Yechezkel 33:15)*, and, "*If there is iniquity in your hand, put it far away; and let not sin dwell in your tent. Then you would lift your face without blemish; you would be steadfast and never fear" (Iyov 11:14,15)*.

The fifth: To contemplate the grandeur of the Creator against Whose word you rebelled by leaving His service and casting aside the teachings of His Torah. You should rebuke yourself for that, as it says, "*Is this the way you repay God?" (Devarim 32:6)*, and, "*'Do you not fear Me?' says Hashem" (Yirmeyah 5:22)*.

This completes the discussion of the specifics of repentance.

CHAPTER SIX

Things That Motivate a Person to Repent

A person can be motivated to repent four ways:

The first person repents after becoming intensely aware of God's greatness and His infinite kindness; he realizes that it is his obligation to serve God, observe His mitzvos, and refrain from the things He prohibited. We can compare this person to a servant who ran away from his master, but after contemplating how good the master had treated him, voluntarily returns and asks forgiveness for running away. This servant who chooses of his own accord to do the right thing, deserves to be forgiven.

Concerning one who returns to God in this manner it says, "*'If you repent, O Israel,' said God, 'you will return to Me'*" *(Yirmeyah 5:22)*, which means, "If you repent of your own free will, before you are punished, I will accept your repentance and choose you for My service." The passage continues, "*If you remove your abominations from before Me, without straying [from My service]; if you swear by My Name in truth, in justice, and in righteousness,*" meaning, if you are sincere about returning to Me, then, *"the nations will bless themselves through [Israel] and will praise themselves through [Israel]*, meaning, I will elevate you to such heights of good fortune that people will bless each other, "*May you be like an Israelite.*" The entire concept is summed up in the verse, "*Return to Me, and I will return to you*" *(Malachi 3:7)*.

Motivation through Reproof

The second person, repents when he hears the Creator's admonition for his wrongdoing. He may hear this rebuke from a prophet—if he lived in the era of the prophets—or he himself may read the reproof in the Torah, or he may be reprimanded by a spiritual leader who exhorts the people to serve God. There are outstanding leaders in every generation, who do so. This in turn, enables God to reproach His people for their failure to repent. As our Sages said, "Before Moshe's sun had set, the sun of Yehoshua, his student, had risen. Before Eli's sun had set, the sun of Shmuel of Ramah had risen. Before Eliyahu's sun had set, the sun of Elisha had risen. And on the day Rabbi Akiva died, Rabbi Yehudah Hanassi was born" (Kiddushin 72b). It has been like that throughout our history, wherever Jews have lived. In every generation there are righteous leaders who urge the people to serve God and who teach them His Torah.

One inspired to repentance by admonition, is like a servant who ran away from his master, and then met another loyal servant who reproached him for running away and advised him to return, assuring him that his master would forgive him, by reminding him how kind the master had been to him. The servant thereupon returned to the master and humbled himself before him.

Motivation By the Punishment of Others

The third person, repents when he notices the punishment G-d inflicts on people who follow the path he has taken. Seeing others suffer, he returns to God out of fear of punishment. One driven to repentance by fear of Divine retribution, is like a servant who ran away from his master and learned of the punishment another fugitive servant received. Chastened by what he heard, he returned to his master, begging forgiveness. As it says, "*Do not cause the land to vomit you out when you defile it, as it vomited out the nation that was there before you*" *(Vayikra 18:28).*

Motivated By Punishment

The fourth person, repents after God punishes him by bringing suffering upon him. Due to his troubles he wakes up and repents of his failings. He is like a servant who ran away from his master and was visited by an agent who disciplined him for evading his duties. Whereupon, the servant returned to his master, confessed his wrongdoing and begged to be forgiven. Of people like this [who repent only when they see punishment staring them in the face], it says, "*When your fear arrives as sudden darkness, and misfortune comes like a storm; when affliction and oppression come upon you, then they will call Me, but I will not answer" (Mishlei 1:27,28).* This was the repentance of King Menasheh, as it says, "*But in his distress he beseeched Hashem , his God, and he humbled himself greatly before the God of his fathers. He prayed to Him, and He was entreated by him and heard his supplication" (2 Divrei Hayamim 33:12,13).*

Summary

The first penitent, who repented [by self motivation], achieves the supreme form of repentance. Less acceptable is the repentance of he who repents only after hearing the rebuke of the Creator. Still less favored and acceptable is the person who does not repent until misfortune strikes those around him. Least favored is the person who does not repent until he himself has been punished and made to suffer. His repentance will not be accepted until he shows remorse, turns away from sin, and asks forgiveness in such a way that he deserves to have his repentance accepted and his transgressions overlooked.

CHAPTER SEVEN

Deterrents to Repentance

There are many things that stand in the way of repentance. I already mentioned most of them in previous chapters of this Gate.

But I want to add another factor, which is, committing yourself to sin; continually sinning and desisting from changing your bad conduct. If you behave like this, you cannot repent. As the saying has it: "No sin is small if you persist in doing it; no sin is great if you ask forgiveness for it." If you keep sinning, you show contempt for the word of God, sneering at His *mitzvos* and punishments. About such a person it says, "*If a person acts highhandedly . . . he is blaspheming God, for he scorned the word of God" (Bamidbar 15:30,31).*

Furthermore, if you repeat the sin—no matter how small it may be—it grows and becomes a greater sin. Conversely, if you committed a great sin, and beg forgiveness and stop doing it out of fear of God, it will get smaller, until it is erased completely from the book of your transgressions, and you will be cleansed of it through your repentance.

Think of silk thread. Consider how strong it becomes when you double it over a number of times, yet it started out as a weak filament, made of the excretions of a silkworm. By contrast, a ship's heavy cable, gradually frays after prolonged use, eventually tears, and becomes useless. The same applies to sin. The smallest sin grows big if you keep doing it; the biggest sin becomes small if you stop doing it and ask forgiveness for it. That is why the verse compares sin to a rope, saying, "*Woe to those who pull iniquity upon themselves with cords of falsehood, and sin like the ropes of a wagon*" *(Yeshayah 5:18)*. In the same vein, we have a saying: "Don't look at the smallness of your sin but at the greatness of the One you sinned against. Do not rejoice over the fact that people are unaware of the evil within you, rather lament because the Creator is aware of what you are hiding. For you forget, but He does not forget; you overlook, but He does not overlook. As it says, '*Behold, it is inscribed before Me' (Yeshayah 5:60)*, and, '*The sin of Yehudah is inscribed with an iron pen' (Yirmeyah 17:1)*."

BACKSLIDING

Another factor standing in the way of repentance is relapsing after you have repented and stopped sinning completely. As it says, "*The word that came to Yirmeyah from Hashem, . . . 'that every man set free his Hebrew slaves—both male and female . . .' But they reneged after that and took back the bondsmen and the men and women they had set free, and forced them into slavery again" (Yirmeyah 34:8-11)*.

PUTTING OFF REPENTANCE

A further barrier to repentance is promising to repent later, planning to stop transgressing after you have gratified your lusts. That would amount to cheating God. As our Sages said, "A person who says, 'I will sin and repent; I will sin [again], and repent [again],' will not be given an opportunity to repent" (Yoma 85b).

In the Words of Reproof that appear at the end of this book I write as follows:

> O my soul, prepare abundant provisions, do not stint,
> While you are still alive and able,
> For a long journey lies ahead of you.

Do not say, "I will prepare tomorrow,"
For the day is fading,
And you never know what tomorrow may bring.
Remember, yesterday will not come back,
And whatever you did,
Will be weighed, counted and measured.
Do not say, "I will do it tomorrow,"
For the day of death
Is hidden from every living being.
Hurry to do each day's assignment,
For death's arrows and lightning bolts
Are streaking all the time.
Do not tarry doing your day's task,
For like a bird roaming from its nest,
Man must go forth from his place [in this world].

Selective Repentance

Yet another impediment to repentance is repenting of some of your sins while persisting in others. For example, refraining from sinning against God and repenting of it, but continuing to sin against man by robbing, cheating, and the like. As it says, "*If there is iniquity in your hand, put it far away*" *(Iyov 11:14)*.

And our Sages (Taanis 16a) said, "A person who sinned and confesses his sin but does not repent, [from all his sins,] may be compared to a man who immerses himself while holding a dead reptile. Even were he to immerse in all the waters of the world, his immersion would be useless. But once he throws the reptile away, his immersion is effective, as it says, "*One who confesses and forsakes [his sins] will be granted mercy*" *(Mishlei 28:13)*.

The negative influences mentioned in the previous Gates are also deterrents to repentance, but there is no need to reiterate them here.

CHAPTER EIGHT

Is One Who Repents Equal to a *Tzaddik*

Some people who have repented are on an equal footing with righteous people who have never sinned; others are on a higher plane than righteous people; still others, in spite of their repentance, rank lower than righteous people.

Equal to a *Tzaddik*

An example of the first category is someone who sinned by failing to fulfill a positive commandment which is not punishable by *kares*—premature death,—like *tzitzis, lulav, sukkah*, and the like. If this person repents in his heart and with words, fulfills the mitzvah, and does not ignore it again, the Creator will forgive him. He is considered equal to a righteous person who has never neglected these mitzvos. About him it is said, "He who repents of a sin is like one who never sinned." And our Sages point out, "If you neglect to do a positive mitzvah that is not punishable by kares, and repent, you will be forgiven even before you have moved from your place" (Yoma 86a), as it says, "*Return to Me, and I will return to you" (Malachi 3:7).*

On a Higher Plane Than the *Tzaddik*

An example of the second category—someone who ranks higher than the *tzaddik*—is a person who violated a minor negative commandment which is not punishable by *kares* and repents of it completely, complying with all the particulars of repentance. He bears his sin in mind all the time, constantly asks forgiveness for it and is filled with shame before the Creator. He is brokenhearted and humbles himself constantly before God. His sin has become the impetus for his submission to God and his attempt to repay his debt to the Creator. He will not become proud of his good deeds nor will he consider them great; he is careful not to stumble in sin the rest of his life.

Such a sinner is on a higher plane than a *tzaddik* who never committed that or a comparable sin. For you cannot be sure that the *tzaddik* will not become haughty and self-satisfied. As a popular saying has it, "Some sins are more helpful to the one who repents than all the righteous deeds of the *tzaddik*; and some righteous deeds are more harmful to the *tzaddik* than all the sins of the penitent." This can happen to a *tzaddik* when he throws submissiveness overboard and becomes obsessed with pride.

A *tzaddik* once said to his students, "If you were free of sin, I would worry that you were guilty of something worse than sin."

"But what could be worse than sin?" they asked.

"Pride and hypocrisy," he replied.

The Sages had this kind of *baal teshuvah* in mind when they said, "*Where a baal teshuvah stands, even a perfect tzaddik cannot stand*" *(Berachos 34b)*.

Lower Than a *Tzaddik*

The third category pertains to a person who violated major negative commandments which are punishable by the death penalty or *kares*, such as desecration of God's Name, swearing falsely, or the like. He then repented fully, complying with all the details of repentance. Nevertheless, he can not attain forgiveness until he is put through trials in this world that test the limits of his endurance. Our Sages had such a *baal teshuvah* in mind when they said (Yoma 86A), "If someone violates a negative commandment that is punishable by *kares* or execution and repents, pain and agony cleanse him, and death brings forgiveness, as it says, "*Then I will punish their transgression with the rod, and their iniquity with plagues" (Tehillim 89:33)*, and, "*This sin will never be atoned for until you die" (Yeshayah 22:14)*.

The *tzaddik* who never committed such transgressions, undoubtedly ranks higher than the one who repents of them.

CHAPTER NINE

Can a Sinner Repent of Any Sin

There are two kinds of sins: Those committed against God in which the sinner hurts no one but himself, and is only guilty of rebelling against the commandments of God. These include denying His existence, thinking immoral thoughts and holding heretical views, violating the "duties of the heart" [like being jealous, hating, and coveting], as well as transgressing the "duties of the limbs" [mitzvos like *tefillin, tzitzis, matzah, shofar, and sukkah*].

The second kind of sin is committed against your fellow man. These include injuring them bodily, causing damage to their property, or ruining their reputation. With these sins, you hurt yourself by rebelling against God, and you harm others as well.

Sins Against God

You can repent of sins committed against God alone, if you become aware of your shortcomings and show remorse before Him. Common sense tells you that you to repent the way you sinned, if possible. For example, if you violated one of the mitzvos in the category of "duties of the heart," like having disloyal beliefs in your heart and mind, or bearing a grudge against someone, repent by becoming goodhearted, rejoicing in other people's good fortune, and being forgiving toward others. If you sinned with your body, by eating forbidden foods, having forbidden sexual relations, desecrating Shabbos or Yom Tov, or taking a false oath, repent by trying to offset the sinful act you were guilty of, doing it in a spirit of dedication to God.[1]

This you can do as long as you live, provided your mind is clear when you decide to repent and cleanse your soul of your sin. As the wise Shlomoh said, *"If you have become wise, you have become wise for your own good" (Mishlei 9:12).*

Sins Against God and Man

But if you sinned against God and your fellow man,[2] repentance becomes difficult for several reasons: the victim may have died or moved away; you may have lost the money you misappropriated and have no way to make restitution, your victim may not be willing to forgive you for the harm you caused to his person, or for the slander you spread about him. Perhaps you may not know your victim, or the amount you defrauded if, for example, you embezzled money from a community fund or government agency, and do not know how much you took. Maybe the money in question became mixed with your own, and you can not separate it without major loss. As our Sages said, "If a person stole a beam and used it in the construction of a palace, Beis Shammai says that he must tear down the building and return the beam to its owner; but Beis Hillel says that he must pay only the value of the beam, in order to encourage pilferers to repent" (Gittin 55a).

---

[1] For example, if a person ate forbidden foods, he should refrain from indulging in sumptuous meals and limit himself to small quantities of simple food (Pas Lechem).

[2] Every sin against your fellow is inherently a sin against God, because the Torah forbids harming others (Pas Lechem).

Other Cases When Repentance is Difficult

It is difficult to repent when you have become so used to doing a sin that it is in your blood, like any habit to which you are addicted. As it says, "*They train their tongue to speak falsehood, striving to be iniquitous" (Yirmeyah 9:4)*, "*Can a Cushite change his skin [color], or a leopard his spots?* " *(ibid. 13:23)*.

It is difficult to repent of bloodshed, or the slaying of innocent people, whether through violence or slander, such as the case of Doeg and the city of kohanim. He first tried to have the kohanim murdered by slandering them, and then he himself killed them in cold blood, as it says, "*Doeg the Edomite circled around and killed the kohanim" (1 Shmuel 22:18)*.

It is also difficult to repent if you caused someone to lose money because you spread false rumors about him. In such a case repentance does not help unless you appease your victim by compensating him and humbly asking his forgiveness, as it says, "*You have eaten the flesh of My people, you have stripped their skin from upon them. You have broken open their bones . . . Then they will cry out to Hashem, but He will not answer them" (Michah 3:3,4)*.

It is also difficult when a person engages in forbidden sexual relations with a woman who then gives birth to an illegitimate child. It is impossible to correct this disgrace, because the stain can never be washed away, as it says, *For that is licentiousness; that is an iniquity for the judges [to punish]! For it is a fire; it consumes unto doom" (Iyov 31:11,12)*, and, "*They betrayed Hashem, begot alien children" (Hoshea 5:7)*.

Repentance is also difficult for someone who habitually spreads lies, false rumors and makes fun of people, because such a person can never keep track of what he said; there is no end to it, and he does not remember whom he maligned. All this is recorded and stored in the book of his wrongdoing. As it says, "*If one comes to visit, insincerely does he speak, his heart gathers iniquity for himself; upon going out he speaks it" (Tehillim 41:7)* [which Rashi explains, If one of my enemies comes to visit me in my sickness, he pretends to be my friend while actually he is scheming to malign me. And when he leaves, he slanders me]. It says furthermore, "*If you saw a thief, you agreed to be with him, and with adulterers was your lot. You dispatched your mouth for evil, and your tongue adheres to deceit. You sit and speak against your brother, you slander your mother's son*" *(ibid. 50:18-20)*. The verse equates gossiping, with stealing and adultery. It says also, "*Everyone mocks his neighbor*" *(Yirmeyah 9:4)*.

It is most difficult to repent if a person leads others astray by inventing his own religion and brainwashing people to believe in it. He transgresses and makes others transgress. The more people he seduces, the guiltier he is. As our Sages say, "Whoever influences the masses to become righteous will not stumble into sin; but one who influences the masses to sin can never repent . . . . Yaravam sinned and caused the masses to sin, so the sin of the masses is charged against him, as it says, '*For the sins of Yaravam which he committed, and which he caused Israel to commit' (1 Melachim 15:30)*" *(Avos 5:18)*.

Included in this category is a person who is in a position to guide people to do good and keep them from evil, but passes up the opportunity because he wants their money, or is afraid or too bashful to admonish them. Because he did not show them the right way, they continue to sin, and he is blamed as it says, "*He is wicked and will die for his iniquity, but I will demand his blood from your hand*" *(Yechezkel 33:18)*.

CHAPTER TEN

ADVICE FOR A PERSON WHO FINDS IT DIFFICULT TO REPENT

Sins that are difficult to correct by repenting in the way that is appropriate for that transgression are either offenses against God, or offenses against other men.

If you cannot repent for any of the reasons mentioned earlier, but nonetheless undertake to abide by all the main points and particulars of repentance, the Creator makes repentance easier for you. He disregards the things you are unaware of, paving the way toward repentance, and making generous allowances for you.

For example, if a person engaged in forbidden sexual relations and fathered an illegitimate child, the Creator will cause the offspring to die.

If your sin involved fraud, God will see to it that you have the means to repay the victim and make amends, so that he forgives you. If you injured someone or tarnished his name, the Creator will fill your victim's heart with cordiality and generosity, so that he forgives you for the harm you caused him, as it says, "*When Hashem favors a man's way, even his foes will make peace with him*" *(Mishlei 16:7)*. If the injured party moved away, the Creator will have the two of you meet, giving you the opportunity to humble yourself before him, so he can forgive you. If you do not know whom you have defrauded nor the amount involved, God will arrange that you donate money to a communal project like building bridges, digging wells for public use, or installing wells along roads where there is no drinking water, or similar public works, so that your victim and everyone else will enjoy them.

If the person you wronged died, [God will enable you] to return the money to his heirs. If you injured him or maligned him publicly, you should confess at his grave before ten men, and you will be forgiven. As our Sages say, "Take ten men to the grave and say, 'I have sinned against God, the God of Israel and against so-and-so, whom I have injured" (Yoma 87a).

In the final analysis, the only thing that keeps a sinner from repenting is his evil impulse and his treacherous heart. For the gate of repentance is never closed, and nothing can stop one who sincerely want to draw closer to God. On the contrary, God will open for him the gate of virtue and show him the good path, as it says, "*It is something that is very close to you" (Devarim 30:14)*, and, "*Hashem is close to all who call upon Him, to all who call upon Him sincerely" (Tehillim 145:18).*

A Fervent Plea

Dear brother, Now that I have explained your obligation to repent, and have shown you how to repent, you have no excuse for failing to repent. Any defense you offer will be rejected.

What will you say to God tomorrow? Will you say, "I didn't know that I had to repent"? You did know! Will you say, "I confess to what I did, but I didn't know how to repent"? [That excuse is not valid either, because I showed you how to repent.] How will you answer the question we are asked in the hereafter, "Why did you not repent?" Prepare your answer while you still have time. But remember, brother, that your response will be measured by your deeds, not by your words.

Contemplate on how you can find favor with your Creator. For only he who hastens will savor the good today, and the fruit of negligence is self-reproach.

Wake up from your sleep, foolish brother, and have pity on your soul, the precious treasure the Creator entrusted to you. How much longer will you wait before you repent? You have wasted your life so far gratifying your passion, like a runaway servant. Should you not return and spend the rest of your life pleasing your Creator? You know that life is short, and what is left of your life is even shorter. As our Sages said, "*The day is short, but the task is abundant*" *(Avos 2:15)*.

Brother, you have a noble soul, but you used it to pay homage to the values of this worthless, fleeting, material world, ignoring your destiny in the everlasting hereafter. Set your spiritual sights upward, toward that glorious place, that lofty dwelling on High, where souls soar ever higher, never to descend.

Hurry, while [you are still alive and] the gate of repentance is open, and your repentance will be accepted and forgiveness will be granted, as it says, "*Seek Hashem when He can be found, call upon Him when He is near*" *(Yeshayah 55:6)*. Hurry, brother, before your fears are realized, for you don't know if you will last the day! Do some serious soul-searching and analyze your actions as best you can. Whoever wants to find favor with his Creator has to enter the narrow door which the long-suffering pious men enter. While we all aspire to the good, only those who run swiftly to it will attain it. As our Sages said, "Be bold as a leopard, light as an eagle, swift as a deer, and strong as a lion, to carry out the will of your Father in Heaven" (Avos 5:20), and as David said, "*I hastened and did not delay to keep Your commandments*" *(Tehillim 119:60)*.

Search you soul, and hang your head in shame for behaving toward your Creator in a way you would not behave toward your fellow human being. If you enrage even a minor government official, you would not wait a minute to humble yourself before him, pleading with him to forgive you and not punish you, although he has no say in the matter. You surely would demean yourself if an influential minister was angry with you, let alone, the king himself. Fearing his prompt punishment, you would rush to ask his forgiveness, repenting and trying to placate him, even though you knew that he cannot do anything unless the Creator decreed it, as the wise Shlomoh said, "*Like streams of water is the heart of kings in the hand of Hashem, wherever He wishes, so He directs it" (Mishlei 21:1)*. His reign may come to an end or he may be overthrown before he can punish you. He has many things on his mind, and in all likelihood may lose sight of what you have done, because he overlooks many obvious things, not to mention hidden things. Although you know all this, you do not wait a minute to beg his forgiveness.

So how can you not be ashamed before your Creator, Who sees both your hidden and visible deeds and thoughts, Who neither forgets nor overlooks, Who is never distracted, Whose judgment no one can escape, Whose reign is everlasting! How can you turn away from Him and stall for time before being submissive to Him and repenting before Him, when you do not know when your life will end, and how long you are destined to live?

If someone were to warn the inhabitants of a city, saying, "Folks! Get ready to travel to the World to Come! One of you will pass away this month, though I don't know who." Everyone would prepare to die, for fear that it may be he who will be chosen. Then why are we not prepared, seeing that death indeed takes many from us every month? Common sense tells us to prepare the provisions for our dwelling place in the hereafter. [Shouldn't we make these preparations] at least one day before we die? As our Sages said, "Repent one day before your death" (Avos 2:10), and, "*Let your garments always be white" (Koheles 9:8)*—[meaning you should always be in spiritual readiness].

Clarify the truth of this by your observation, confirm it with your own intelligence rather than depending only on what others tell you. Do not dismiss the conclusions you reach with your own mind [that you should make preparations for life in the hereafter]. The Creator does many favors for His servants; if they accept them, they will benefit, but if they reject them, they will be punished. To be specific, the Creator has blessed you with the gifts of wisdom, understanding, and knowledge, making you superior to other creatures through it. Be very careful that these gifts should not incriminate you [for ignoring their advice]! God urges you [through His prophets] to follow the straight path and shows you the road to happiness out of His compassion for you. He guides you at a moderate pace, making repentance easy for you, because He does not want you to continue acting senselessly and defiantly [pursuing hollow material values]. He wants to treat you with kindness, as befits God Who is compassionate and merciful toward all His creatures, as it says, "*Good and upright is Hashem, therefore He guides sinners on the way [to repentance]*" *(Tehillim 25:8)*.

He calls out to you, to repent; at first speaking gently, then scolding and shaming you, and finally threatening you with punishment, in order that you repent and quickly return to Him.

Make haste, my brother, to listen and become close to Him. Choose for your soul what God Himself has chosen for it; demand of it what your Creator demands of it. Don't be nonchalant about this; if your own soul seems trifling to you, what do you deem important?

You may say, "I have neglected to serve God the better part of my life—how can I return to God now and ask Him to forgive me?" Your should answer like the prophet who said, "*If a righteous person turns away from his righteousness and does wrong . . . shall he live? And if a wicked person turns back from the wickedness he practiced and does what is just and right, he shall live; he shall not die*" *(Yechezkel 18:21-24)*.

The early Sages compared a person who repents late in life to a man who had many coins and had to cross a river. Standing on the riverbank, he threw his coins into the river, trying to dam it up [but was unsuccessful]. When he had one coin left, he said to the captain of a passing boat, "Take the one coin I have left, and take me across the river in your boat." The captain agreed, and the man accomplished with his last coin what he could not accomplish with all the coins he had thrown into the river. [Because he accomplished the transfer,] it seemed as if he had not lost anything [by throwing all the coins in the river].

The same goes for a penitent who wasted his life doing everything except serving God. When he repents at the end of his life, the Creator forgives him all the transgression he committed throughout his life, as it says, "*None of the transgression he committed shall be remembered against him*" (*Yechezkel 18:22*), and, "*None of the sins he committed shall be remembered against him*" (*ibid. 33:16*).

Do not be upset, my brother, that I am urging you to guard yourself, because you neglected to act properly for such a long time. My words are meant for myself as well. Yield to the truth rather than evade it. Thank God for making you aware of things you did not know until now. Do not use as an excuse the fact that the person who is encouraging you to repent has himself neglected the service of God for a long time. That thought is a ruse and trap the *yetzer hara* uses to lure people with weak discernment.

May God, in His mercy, place us among those who are quick to repent and return to Him with sincerity. Amen.

GLOSSARY

ASHERA - Tree planted for idol worship
BAALEI TESHUVA - penitants
BAMIDBAR - The Book of Numbers
BEREISHIS - The Book of Genesis
DEVARIM - The Book of Deuteronomy
DIVREI HAYAMIM - The Book of Chronicles
EICHA - The Book of Lamentations
GEMARA - Talmud
IYOV - Job
KARES - punishment of premature death
KOHEIN pl. *KOHANIM* - Priests, descendants of Aaron
KOHELES - Ecclesiastes
LULAV - palm branch take on Sukkos
MELACHIM - The Book of Kings
MEZUZAH - scroll containing the Shema that is placed on the doorpost.
MISHLEI - Proverbs
SHEMOS - The Book of Exodus
SHMONA ESREI - The silent prayer said three times daily
SHOFAR - Ram's horn blown on Rosh Hashana
SUKKAH - hut used on Tabernacles
TAANAIM AND AMORAIM - Sages of the Mishnah and Talmud
TEFILLIN - phylacteries
TEHILLIM - Psalms
TZADDIK pl. *TZADDIKIM* - Righteous people
TZITZIS - fringes worn on a four cornered garment
VAYIKRA - The Book of Leviticus
YECHEZKEL - Ezekiel
YEHOSHUA - Joshua
YESHAYAH - Isaiah
YETZER HARA - evil inclination
YIRMIYAH - Jeremiah
YOEL - Joel
YONAH - Jonah